RELIGION IN
CONTEMPORARY EUROPE

Edited by

John Fulton

and

Peter Gee

Texts and Studies in Religion
Volume 64

The Edwin Mellen Press
Lewiston/Queenston/Lampeter

BL
695
.R43
1994

Library of Congress Cataloging-in-Publication Data

Religion in contemporary Europe / edited by John Fulton and Peter Gee.
    p.   cm.
    Includes bibliographical references and index.
    ISBN 0-7734-9028-0
    1. Europe--Religion--20th century.   I. Fulton, John, Dr.
II. Gee, Peter.
BL695.R43   1994
200'.94'09049--dc20   94-21169
                                                        CIP

This is volume 64 in the continuing series
Texts and Studies in Religion
Volume 64 ISBN 0-7734-9028-0
TSR Series ISBN 0-88946-976-8

A CIP catalog record for this book is available from the British Library.

Copyright © 1994 The Edwin Mellen Press

All rights reserved. For information contact

The Edwin Mellen Press   The Edwin Mellen Press
        Box 450   Box 67
Lewiston, New York   Queenston, Ontario
USA 14092-0450   CANADA L0S 1L0

The Edwin Mellen Press, Ltd.
Lampeter, Dyfed, Wales
UNITED KINGDOM SA48 7DY

Printed in the United States of America

RELIGION IN
CONTEMPORARY EUROPE

Contents

Acknowledgements

The driving force from which this book grew was a conference at St Mary's College, Strawberry Hill, in the Spring of 1991. Three people on behalf of their academic associations originated the conference: Kim Knott of the British Association for the Study of Religion, Ken Medhurst of the British Political Science Association's group of religion specialists, and most of all, Grace Davie, then Secretary of the British Sociological Associations's Sociology of Religion Study Group, who convened the working party and carried through the agenda for the conference 'Religion in the Common European Home'. John Fulton was the local organiser of the conference and, with Peter Gee, took over the project after the conference until its conclusion, through selection of themes and authors to the editing and production of the present volume. All three associations have expressed particular thanks to those who have borne the project, and particularly to Grace and John.

This book forms the second in what promises to become a regular feature in the field of social studies of religion in Britain, the first being Peter Gee and John Fulton (1991). A third volume, edited by Kieran Flanagan and Peter Jupp and dealing with the theme 'Religion and Modernity', is expected to appear in the following year.

Contributors

Ahmed Andrews, Department of Sociology, University of Aberdeen, Scotland

Régine Azria, Ecole des Hautes Etudes en Sciences Sociales, University of Paris, France

James Beckford, Department of Sociology, University of Warwick, Coventry, England

Grace Davie, Department of Sociology, University of Exeter, England

Jon Davies, Department of Religious Studies, University of Newcastle, England

John Fulton, Department of Sociology, St Mary's College, Strawberry Hill, Twickenham, England

Peter Gee, Overseas Development Institute, London, England

Danièle Hervieu-Léger, Ecole des Hautes Etudes en Sciences Sociales, University of Paris, France

Patrick Michel, Ecole des Hautes Etudes en Sciences Sociales, University of Paris, France

David Martin, Department of Sociology, London School of Economics, England

Richard Roberts, Director, Institute for Religion and the Human Sciences, St Mary's College, University of St Andrews, St Andrews, Scotland

Petya Nitzova, Bulgarian Academy of Sciences, Sofia, Bulgaria and Hartford Seminary, Connecticut, USA

Liliane Voyé, Catholic University of Louvain, Louvain–la–Neuve, Belgium

Michael Watson, Department of International Politics, University College Aberystwyth, Wales

Jean-Paul Willaime, Ecole Pratique des Hautes Etudes, University of Paris and Director, Centre de Sociologie Comparée des Religions en Europe, Université des Sciences Humaines, Strasbourg, France

Introduction
John Fulton

The dramatic changes which have been taking place in the whole world order in the years since 1989 have their roots in the programme of *Glasnost* forced on the Soviet Union by Mikhail Gorbachev from 1985, which culminated in the collapse of communism in the Eastern bloc countries and the disaggregation of the Soviet Union. The re-unification of Germany and the pressure on the EC to accommodate this, as well as the clamourings of Eastern European countries for aid, help and consideration for a place under the European sun, signify that Europe as a whole is going to be re-shaped from within over the next few decades. The prognosis is unclear and stretches from Gorbachev's friendly consideration of a 'common European home' to fears of destabilisation, as war splits the Balkans and the Caucuses, the Kurdish question re-emerges in Turkey and Iraq, and old ethnic conflicts hold their course in Northern Ireland and Spain. The euphoria at the collapse of the Berlin Wall has been replaced with political fudging as people blame the UN for 'mishandling' aid to the Balkans and involvement in Somalia, and the world economy, Europe included, undergoes its worst crisis since the 1930s.

Indeed, as Western Europe views men, women and children slaughtered in Eastern Europe with as much ferocity as that experienced under the Third Reich, this time because they belong to yet other ethno-religious groups, old patterns of conflict re-emerge to challenge facile arguments on the increasing humanity of

European society, and some even look back with a degree of romanticism to the peace established by the Soviet regime and Tito's Yugoslavia.

Clearly there is more to Europe than the false but welcome peace which came to it and endured for forty-five years after the defeat of nazism. Previous issues have re-emerged and have to be resolved, just as local populations have become empowered to the use of the gun as well as the ballot box. One such non-marginal issue is the role of religion in the new Europe, whatever the shape of that Europe turns out to be. The fact that religion is historically related to ethnicity and has interacted with the growth of national identities means that it cannot be ignored by anyone seeking to make sense of the political maze with which Europe presents us today. How religious factors relate to conflicts, to national and ethnic identities, the place they have in cultures, and their ability to motivate both aggression and pacification, to side with dominant powers or with the subordinated: how religious factors do all this within a European context has to be explored if the future lines of Europe are to be discerned and if one is to construct public policies and internationally organised responses appropriate to the circumstances.

What the authors of this book hope to do is to illuminate central European problems and situations in which religion plays a role. The book fills a gap, filled in part by the Journal *Religion State and Society* for much of what has been happening in the Eastern bloc, but for which no other journal has provided information so far as the rest of Europe is concerned. David Martin's overview in Chapter 1 is specific rather than general, as he seeks with much success to delineate patterns of religious and other power-source interaction throughout Europe in recent years. He deals synthetically with his topic: the gradual disentanglement of Protestantism and Catholicism from state involvement in the West, and of the state and other political secularisms from ethnic cultures; the decomposition of Western state nationalisms and the emergence of especially Eastern micro-nationalisms linked to religious identities: in the Ukraine, Armenia, Azerbaijan, the former Yugoslavia; and the European-wide occurrence of 'oppression exercised by the oppressed against their own minorities'. The role of religion both in revolution and in the affirmation of the new identities is clearly identified.

Chapter 2 by Richard Roberts confronts the input which religion and religious thinkers have made both to the definition of the contours of Europe and to images of its prevailing culture. He examines the concepts of Europe of the recent past: the Christendom tradition of interpretation from Christopher Dawson to Pope John Paul II, Orientalism as the counterpoint of an attempted European cultural dominance of the Islamic world, Troeltsch's view of Protestantism as the dominant driving force of culture within Europe, and Spengler's deconstruction of all such theories. Roberts uses Robertson's globalisation theory to debunk all those politically constructed changes which are driven by belief in a purposive form of modernisation.

Chapters 3 and 4 look at religion's present input to Eastern European societies. Patrick Michel (Chapter 3) examines the interaction between Roman Catholicism and emerging state institutions in Poland, Hungary, the Czech Republic and Slovakia. He examines the ways in which religion and the churches operated as a vector for the steady release of these countries from Soviet domination. He points up the difficulties religious institutions are now having in finding an appropriate place in the newly emerging capitalist democracies. In Poland, the pluralism advocated by Mazowiecki is strongly combatted by the Catholic-centred nationalism of Walesa and Cardinal Glemp. In Hungary and Czechoslovakia the status of the church is seen to be rapidly declining after its high position at the point of revolution. Michel stresses there is still no strategy to succeed the oppositional form which was the emblem of resistance to communism. Normative conformity is still sought rather than pluralisation.

In Chapter 4, Petya Nitzova looks at Islam's long-standing indigenous presence in Europe and its relationship to Christians – of direct relevance to the current crises in South Eastern Europe. There is a long standing sense among Christians of cultural superiority to Muslims and a derogatory attitude which can be traced back to the eighth century. But despite the opposition of classic Islam and Christianity, the popular versions of both have frequently experienced affinities in these lands, particularly in their stress on emotional religious forms and the cult of the saints. There has been syncretism in the former Yugoslavian territories from the middle ages, with similar developments in Albania and Bulgaria. Nitzova predicts a return to mutual respect and tolerance once current conflicts have subsided.

Chapters 5, 6 and 7 examine religion in Western Europe. Grace Davie maps out the development of modernity's impact on religion in identifiably different groupings of nation-states, pointing up the crucial difference which Islamic migrations imply for the developing cultures. She looks at the shared religious heritage ('unity') of Western Europeans who remain 'unchurched rather than simply secular' and notes the extent of other religious minorities spread across countries; she goes on to provide useful data on diversity through a comparison of the reactions in Britain and France to the Rushdie affair and to the wearing in schools of clothing denoting religious identity.

Régine Azria, in Chapter 6, concentrates on the new emergent identity of Jewish communities. She examines the 'Jewish space' the group has created within and throughout European culture from the early middle ages while at the same time acknowledging the accompanying suffering and oppression. The Ashkenazi tradition was of particular European value, until swept away by the Holocaust. Contemporary Jewish identity in Europe has been radically reshaped by the Six Days' War of 1967. But the post-war generation, more emphatically Jewish than their parents were, remains unsure about which specific values should dominate their consciousness.

Ahmed Andrews, in Chapter 7, concentrates on the impact of modernity on Muslim women's rights in a Western European setting. It is often conventionally assumed that women enjoy restricted and limited social status in Islam, yet the author argues that this is not necessarily so. Muslim attitudes towards women vary according to the particular Islamic theological and juridical traditions followed within each community. In an empirical study from Leicester, England, of two Gujurati communities from a similar ethnic background, the different experiences of women in Sunni and Shia mosques are identified, lending some support to the hypothesis that theological differences have a significant impact upon women's social position.

Chapters 8, 9 and 10 tackle the question of European unification and the divergent inputs of the Protestant and Catholic churches. Jean-Paul Willaime considers how the Protestant churches of Europe are seeking to make – or not to make – their impact on the EC and on a future united Europe. He describes in outline the historical development of European Protestantism which, with no central authority, has resulted in a religious provincialism closely linked to national and regional boundaries. Despite this development he shows that linkages between Protestant churches have assumed a growing European dimension. Liberal Protestants have developed an acceptance of secularisation and pluralisation in Europe, combined with opposition to any attempt at a Christian recolonisation of culture. After considering the different position of Protestant fundamentalists, Willaime pinpoints the dilemma confronting European Protestants: to become more centralised so as to speak with one voice, or to remain faithful to Protestant pluralism, and thereby perpetuate Catholic institutional dominance in the new Europe.

Liliane Voyé focuses in Chapter 9 on the Catholic origin of the principle of subsidiarity and its impact on both the European Community and the Roman Catholic Church itself and its internal and external policies. She recognises the current importance of the debates on the concept for European unity, sketching out at the same time its history and formulation by Catholic German theologians in the last half of the nineteenth century. She maps out its application by the papacy to secular society and the papacy's corresponding refusal to apply it to its own church government. She then maps out its application by secular powers and stresses the way regional identities are enabled by the principle while the states themselves continue to experience legitimation crises.

Chapter 10 by Danièle Hervieu-Léger illustrates the difficulty the Pope is having in relaying his own vision of Europe down the line to young French Catholics. She holds that the maintenance of religious identity requires the fostering of collective religious memory, a difficult task in a rapidly changing Europe. The present Papal response has been the 'New Evangelisation' which relies on three main methods: spreading the utopian view of a bygone Christian Europe, an insistence on the maintenance of certain cultural characteristics, and an emotional mobilisation of memory. Hervieu-Léger examines the consequences for a group of some 2,000 French Catholic youth on pilgrimage to Czestochowa, Poland. Direct interpersonal contact and local community experience prove to be the seedbed for their religious identification, and not the Christian Europe of the past desired by the Pope.

Chapters 11 and 12 deal with two opposing inputs to European identity and its future. Jon Davies takes on the impact of war and its memories for Europeans, indicating both the magnitude of the problem it poses for reconciliation and the promise that lies in the same of achieving a conflict-free, plural and tolerant Europe for the future. War has been a dominant factor in the shaping of European consciousness. War memorials have great significance as European symbols. Seen as religious texts, they express a particular Christian version of the heroic epic. Many memorials quote extensively from the Anglican Book of Common Prayer, embodying the Passion story with the Cenotaph as empty tomb. Christian just war doctrine has been buttressed by the theme; monuments are war memorials of it. If cultural identities become synonymous with such enmities, European conflicts will assume serious proportions. But states can assume a new role by controlling these bellicose systems of social identity.

In Chapter 12, Michael Watson looks at the Green Movement and its interaction with Christian tradition and thought. He points out that, with mainstream Christianity still wedded to liberal democracy, pluralism and the market economy, Christian Democracy will continue to dominate Europe as things stand. But, he argues, a 'new politics' is already emerging in concerns such as development and peace issues, minority rights and feminism and, most importantly, ecology. All have a relationship to traditional Christian themes. They can allow religion to claim a modified role, particularly if it rejects the theme of the domination of nature in favour of the key Christian ones of caring and stewardship.

In his *Final Reflections* in Chapter 13, James Beckford indicates the themes from within the book which emerge as possible keys for future frameworks of understanding religion's role in the development of Europe. One the one hand, there is the continuing need to recognise the differing social and theoretical constructs of 'Europe'. On the other lie a set of contrasts: the antinomy of a decline in institutional religious power while boundaries within and at the edge firm up along religious and ethnic lines; the ambiguity of religion as a force both for enmity and peace; the paradox of the growth of minority and local cultures as Europe as an organisation centralises; and finally, the fact that religion was, and is likely to remain, a force coming to Europe from without as well as developing within.

1
Religion in Contemporary Europe[1]
David Martin

This chapter is divided into two main sections. In the first I am principally concerned with broad shifts in the religious situation, more especially various fragmentations and decompositions. In the second I look at changes and conditions in Central and Eastern Europe which reveal the unity of 'the new Europe' and also point up a distinctive situation for the most part created by Soviet and communist domination.

With the passing of the last decade, and specifically with the *annus mirabilis* of 1989, we may be approaching the decomposition of two hundred years and more of statist hostility to religion. In Protestant societies that was expressed more often in cooption, subordination, and subversion; in Catholic societies more often by hostility and partial repression. Religion in Europe is not yet as free of state entanglements as it became in North America between 1620 and 1830, but the old world is, nevertheless, slowly arriving at the condition of the new. The ideologies and secular religions promoting the state and promoted by the state may be merging into practicality. The long shadows cast by Pombal, Joseph II, the Prussian state, the Third Republic, the communist regimes and the Protestant

---

1. This chapter was written in the early Spring of 1992, before the division of Czechoslovakia, and before the collapse of Yugoslavia into ethnic conflicts (*eds*).

erastian establishments, fade into history, leaving secularism as the residual smile on the face of the vanishing cat.

If this decomposition is, indeed, in train, the consequences are likely to be far-reaching. In varying degrees states have pushed back the range of religious activities, they have promoted understandings of religion within evolutionary perspectives, and they have controlled the expression and content of religious faith, especially in education and public media. *Raison d'état*, after all, provided the first secularisation (Willaime 1990:195).

If, as J.P. Williame has suggested, the state is becoming more pragmatic, and more inclined to consult the various spiritual families in French society about matters of common concern, then that opens up a different kind of social space. What chiefly remains from the centuries of enlightened persecution or subversion, or of cultured contempt and indifference, are attitudes lodged in the establishments of education and the modern media. Insofar as these have been agencies for the state they retain the appropriate ideological assumptions and seek to mould a public in the name of progress (Willaime 1990). But, to quote Willaime once more, even in France teachers are tending to transmit knowledge rather than preach progress. And in eastern Europe, of course, the power of organic intellectuals to promote a major version of the enlightenment by force and to implement its attendant theory of secularisation has simply collapsed. In other words, militant secularism may be decomposing in both the western and eastern versions of the enlightenment. A wide variety of beliefs about religion may become permissible even among the intelligentsia.

It might, in parenthesis, be thought that the situation in the Protestant erastian establishments has been very different. After all, these establishments have historically encouraged moralistic versions of religion in order to promote solidarity and social control, and to provide public ceremonial. But Steve Bruce has correctly noted how this lulls religious leaders into a false security, while underneath them the sources of religious reproduction are being undermined. Wherever such religious establishments exist religion becomes regarded as an aspect of status and style, and those who lack the status become unenthusiastic about the religion. There is also inadequate motivation for clergy to secure and defend independent sources of religious socialisation, like Sunday schools, or the education of teachers. Thus, in Britain the so-called conservative governments of 1979–92 were able effectively to remove religious teacher training by reorganising the church colleges inside vast consortia. Attempts by lay Christians of the new right to reintroduce Christian worship within the state schools bolted the door on a long empty stable. Today the main sources of socialisation in schools and media have retreated even from moralism and preach a combination of self-expression, selections from the liberal agenda and environmentalism. It is no wonder the Greens did well in the 1992 schools' general election. This is not secularism, but it is hardly Christianity either, even though many Christians happen to promote environmental consciousness. In Finland, for example, an investigation into what kinds of participation were associated with 'never attending' church put participation in environmental agencies at the top, with 40% (Heino 1991:19).

Of course, the decline of secularism throughout Europe has to do with the unwinding of long-term spirals of mutual hostility. Secularism decomposes into modest practicality as religion releases itself from any direct association with a militant right. But that has been going on for decades. The special feature today is that western communism, as the most militant version of secularism, decomposed overnight and in turn deprived the social system of Catholicism of a major motive for cohesion. The beneficent spiral unwound too fast for Catholic comfort. Catholicism and communism resemble each other in adherence to central control and to doctrine, but also in maintaining extensive networks of patronage. Doctrine goes well with patronage since it offers a rationale for favouritism and nepotism, and especially so when it can point to a nefarious and mortal enemy. On the one hand communism will remain under other names as a system of patronage pursuing opportunist policies intended to pick up sundry discontents. But, on the other hand, the cohesion of the Catholic system and, in particular, its political discipline is undermined by the defeat of its enemies. Thus, in Italy in 1992, the Catholic constituency has small motive to follow the coded advice of the bishops in favour of 'Christian Democracy'. It is the same dilemma as confronts the defence establishments: of whom then are we now afraid?

The partial dissolution of blocs means that all kinds of contents are emerging in kaleidoscopic juxtaposition. Large numbers of people may hold to a postmodern mélange of doubt, of intimations of faith or faiths, and superstition. Of course, the point can be exaggerated, and on matters of fundamental morality and the second half of the Decalogue there seems to be a substantial consensus. One is looking at straws in the wind. In France, for example, young people have abandoned militant secular disbelief concerning a future life, and larger numbers occupy a middle ground embracing neither secure disbelief nor secure faith. In Hungary in 1978 the indices stopped their one-way movement. Flows became eddies.

This increase in incoherence, at least by traditional Christian criteria, has further implications, in particular for the claims of the Roman Catholic Church in the public realm. Even if the incoherence is exaggerated, or was always present, the modern emphasis on individual judgement means that the institutional Church cannot determine either private behaviour or public law. With regard to private behaviour, the key issue is contraception, yet in an overwhelmingly Catholic country like Italy, the birth-rate has fallen below replacement. With regard to public law a key issue is divorce, yet in Italy the Italian electorate voted to legalise divorce.

It is true there are some contrary examples. In Eastern Europe the role of the Catholic Church in bringing down the Polish communist state encouraged some Polish Catholics, most of them lay, to press for a reinstatement of ecclesiastical norms in public law. But it ran, and runs, into massive opposition; and parallel proposals in Hungary encounter even more widespread opposition. The Irish electorate voted against the legalisation of divorce, but even there the legal judgement preventing a fourteen-year-old seeking abortion abroad after being raped had to be rescinded. The Pope may be popular, and in places like Ireland if not in Holland and France, he may be a magnetic symbol, but he has not succeeded in his principal aim of restoring the magisterium. For most Catholics, let alone for others, religious conscientiousness is a personal matter.

Yet the social comment of the churches commands increasing attention, based not on its authority, but on its appeal to humane consensus and on the fund of goodwill the Church possesses on account of good works. In England and Holland, where the churches are numerically weak, they are heard on issues like immigration, the inner city, and poverty. Indeed, on British television and radio during the April 1992 election the Labour leader, Neil Kinnock, named churches first among groups to be consulted about proportional representation. As for Eastern Europe, some of the crucial negotiations prior to the communist overthrow in East Germany were conducted with church leaders as the remaining remnants of civil society. In Czechoslavakia at Christmas 1990, President Havel spoke of the need for truthfulness and 'traditional Christian values'. During the imprisonment of Gorbachev in August 1991, the Moscow Patriarch publicly demanded his release. And, of course, in Poland the Church has spoken in code to and for the whole society throughout the communist period. Yet even in Poland, as everywhere else, it is necessary to distinguish between the Church as promulgating norms to be obeyed, and the Church as sign, as space, as identity, as history, as presence.

Another rather different manifestation of incoherence affecting secularism and Christianity is the weak appeal of what the French call the *Grand Récit*. The sense of a historical narrative with some future consummation seems to have faded in its Christian and Marxist versions, and even in the version postulating scientific progress. Perhaps this is the grain of truth behind dubious assertions of an 'end to history'.

Also significant is the increasing variety of ritual practice and the increasingly subjective motives for church attendance. Individuality implies subjectivisation. The question is not merely how many people attend and how often but the motives for their attendance. It makes a lot of difference if people no longer have a sense of external obligation and of an objective rite achieved by the proper recitation of ritual formulae. In the West people are, in all likelihood, motivated by a search for personal satisfaction; in the East they may seek to be part of a communal presence. If this surmise is correct, it follows that attendance in the West turns on standards and styles of presentation, and these are likely to compare unfavourably with the performances of media professionals elsewhere. Or it may be that what people most devoutly desire is close encounters for healing, for counsel, for fellowship, and for hope. Whatever the nature of the expectation or the search, services are now provided for different markets, for traditionalists, for liberals or for charismatics, and also for those who variously desire encounter, or the performance of a hieratic rite, or sacred music, or opportunity for quiet and meditation. If there is a movement away from the objective, the ritual, and the hieratic, it would follow that the traditional spaces for ritual are no longer appropriate. Clergy literally no longer know what to do with a St. Mark's, Venice or a medieval parish church with nave and chancel. It may also be that they have mistaken the nature of the shifts and offered services to markets that were mainly imaginary.

Texts and hymns exhibit parallel shifts. Texts are revisable and expendable and ecclesiastical officials tune them to what they regard as 'relevant'. The Lord's Prayer ceases to be a universal imprint which can be automatically recited in an agreed version on communal occasions. Hymnody in Protestant societies ceases to be part of the national heritage, and becomes different sets of religious songs used by a variety of publics.

Only the gesture remains universally recognisable, and that is equally true of East and West. In the East the act of crossing oneself or kissing an ikon secures immediate recognition and confers immediate identity, even if you do not recognise the face on the ikon, and such acts have helped religion survive the state-organised discontinuities following 1917. The great pilgrimages have also retained links across the discontinuities. In the contemporary West people light candles even when they no longer know how to pray. Of all the acts of memory the manual act is the most enduring. It remains to be seen what are the enduring manual acts and signs of communism as it in turn survives through its 'little old ladies' and little old gentlemen. After all, they too are disoriented by the loss of a faith, a text, and a hierarchy.

One aspect of fragmentation in Europe is pluralism even though it is routinely exaggerated for political motives and in the service of multiculturalism. The most contentious forms of pluralism come about through migration, above all of Muslims, who upset some on the right because they are the wrong kind of people and some on the left because they hold the wrong kind of views. Though they are an instalment of pluralism for the West they themselves represent a militant identity between a people and a faith. In that sense the pluralism they represent is very ambiguous.

The other aspect of pluralism is not ambiguous and consists in the reinforcement of what up to recently were the small deposits in Europe of evangelical Christianity, some of them with American roots. These reinforcements may actually come from America or they may parallel recent changes there. They remind us that our contemporary cultural field runs from the Rockies to the Urals and that all churches, Catholic and Reformed included, pick up American cultural radiation.

Leaving aside early Baptist and Anabaptist influences, the seedbeds of modern evangelicalism in Europe were planted in the early twentieth century, for example in Romania, Bulgaria, Russia and Sweden. In the East their social provenance remained quite restricted, in part because they were harried and persecuted. But now we see Pentecostal and Baptist churches beginning to expand in Eastern Europe, for example, in Romania. We may be about to witness a take-off of this kind of faith, with considerable neo-Pentecostal infusions having some appeal to the middle class. Nor is the West immune. In Uppsala in Sweden, a neo-Pentecostal church has been remarkably successful in recent years. In Italy the Assemblies of God claim over a quarter of a million members, and modern evangelical churches are even to be observed in southern France.

Latin and Catholic and Orthodox Europe may turn out to be far more open to evangelicalism than is yet realised, as Catholic and secularist domination begins to decompose. If rapid evangelical incursions can occur in Latin America and Quebec, Latin Europe is not necessarily immune. Indeed, the current highly successful evangelical media enterprise in Budapest runs precisely parallel to similar enterprises in São Paulo and Buenos Aires. Popular music, engaging formats, like those in the media and business enterprise, go hand-in-hand, and attract the usual criticisms. We may also expect a series of communal experiments, often with a business component, variously concerned with 'marriage encounter', with therapy under the guidance of trained personnel, and with training in various kinds of expertise. This type of religious enterprise may well encourage economic enterprise. Compared to the older Pentecostalism, it is relatively indifferent to denominational boundaries, and can occur inside as well as outside the mainstream churches. The keynotes are spiritual affinity, close encounter, modernity, and voluntary religious enterprise, much of it in small cells.

The final element of fragmentation leads naturally to a consideration of Eastern Europe. On the one hand it concerns the dissolution of *La Patrie*. Young people in particular are unwilling to be regimented, let alone to immolate themselves, for a country defined by conventional frontiers. The quasi-religious sentiment which galvanised many in the armies of 1914, and was to some extent backed by supporting mobilisations in the Christian churches, is now almost unimaginable, at least in the West. On the other hand, across and within the old frontiers are real foci of attachment, sometimes labelled micro-nationalisms, which are rooted in place, language, and religion, and can inspire ferocious loyalties, at least in the East. Whether in East or West they take fire from each other, so that the example of Lithuania can help ignite any group from Scotland to Tatarstan. They live on mythic histories and historic charters, such as those currently animating and dividing Greeks and Macedonians or Czechs and Slovaks.

In the West the aggressive edge and steady flow of propaganda of micro-nationalism seems to turn around political and economic autonomy and language while the long term historic sentiment is nourished by religion. It is even possible to secure cohesion simply on the basis of locality and economic autonomy, such as animates the Lombard League. Presumably the primacy of political language in the West, even when the pool of historic sentiment is coloured by religion as in Flanders, has something to do with the space allowed in the modern West for political self-expression and the political practicalities involved. In the East, however, nationalities without states have been repressed by every device possible, including mass deportation and mass intrusion of foreign populations. Under such circumstances, nations replenish themselves underground on religious and symbolic resources, and their initial emergence is manifested through shrines and pilgrimages. Thus the first banners of nationalism in the western Ukraine were mingled with the symbols of Uniate Catholicism. The emergent banners of nationalism in Lithuania mingled together the historic symbols of liberty, independence, and the Church. Almost the first act of the new Lithuania as it sought independence was to re-erect the crosses above Vilnius torn down by the Russians. Once the symbolic stake was set up the political practicalities could take centre stage.

Turning to the general situation in Eastern (and Central) Europe) there are several elements which, in combination, give it a distinct character. It is important to stress the *combination* of elements, because these produce something quite distinctive, a new situation. A novel gestalt, combined with a and b and c brings about a new relationship between a and b and c.

Above all, the East has been affected by the removal of the negative association between political power and faith, church and government, which still overhangs the West. Even where the Church was totally taken over and its leadership subsumed or replaced, the decapitation was so obvious and brutal that few were deceived. Of course, the price paid for this release from social bondage was the loss of important means of reproduction, especially schools. Communism now took on all the negative associations of power once borne by the Church, and went further because it denied any transcendental point of reference beyond itself. It attempted to absorb the religious in the political, and even the scientific within the political. Thus when all embracing ideologies as such started to decompose, the victim turned out to be communism and the communist state in hypostatic union.

In Eastern Europe religion had to do no more than exist and survive to constitute an intolerable dissidence, and in some measure to attract other dissidences to itself, including the desire for personal, ethical autonomy, and the sentiment of ethnic autonomy. Freedom and independence gravitated to the open space maintained by the Church. And that meant, for example, that old antagonisms between liberal humanist and Catholic could be set aside, even in Moravia and Bohemia. Patrick Michel has pointed out how in 1968, when socialism with a human 'face' proved impossible, the unlikely union of liberal nationalist and Czech Catholic was consummated. What history set asunder communism joined together. As a Czech nurse commented: in that void it was a choice of 'Drink or believe'. That was why President Havel entered St. Vitus cathedral to receive the blessing of the cardinal-archbishop of Prague. The antagonisms set off by the defeat of Protestantism in 1625, let alone those set off by 1789, were symbolically reversed.

And yet the situation had no need to develop in this way, apart from the logic of total domination in pursuit of utopian illusion. There were several weaknesses in the position of the Church. People often speak as if the massive persecutions and confiscations initiated under the communist enlightenment had little effect. In fact, in Albania and Czechoslavakia, in Hungary, East Germany and Bulgaria, and in parts of the Soviet Union, the influence of religion was greatly curtailed. Even in Catholic Lithuania believers were much reduced in number.

There were plenty of openings for a subtle policy admixed with intermittent brutality and exclusion of Christians from full social participation. Such openings existed where the Soviets had been viewed as liberators, as in Moravia and Bohemia and Bulgaria, or where Catholics could plausibly be linked to clero-fascism as in Croatia and Slovakia. In Protestant countries like East Germany and Estonia, the churches had already been reduced by secularisation to the *de facto* status of voluntary associations. Moreover, in countries of Lutheran and Orthodox traditions, subordination was normal, which is one reason why the *Stasi* could so successfully infiltrate the German Lutheran Church, and why Ceausescu could order the mass re-education of the Romanian clergy. Even in Catholic countries the Josephist tradition of Austria Hungary offered ample opportunities for decapitation. Only Poland was unassailable.

Nevertheless, the desire for ethical independence and ethnic independence did gravitate to the relatively open space maintained by religious faith. First something needs briefly to be said about ethical independence before turning to the complexities of ethnic independence.

Ethical independence was the reverse side of successful decapitation, in East Germany, Hungary, the Soviet Union, and Czechoslovakia. Christian undergrounds emerged in all these countries. In Hungary, for example, there emerged analogues of the base communities with a strong pacifist tinge, and in Czechoslovakia there were many Catholic affiliates of Charter 77. In East Germany the religious underground took up the kind of issue that might avoid direct confrontation. They drew attention to pollution, which the government declared a specifically capitalist phenomenon. They criticised the prevailing militarism and preached love and non-violence rather than class hatred. Gradually, from the late seventies on they extended the space for discussion until it broadened into the vast demonstrations of 1989 around the Nikolaikirche in Leipzig. At that time Christians acted as ushers for the crowds. They pleaded for the avoidance of all acts which might excuse recourse to the tanks visibly available in the side streets. They even offered refuge to Honecker after his fall from power.

As for ethnic independence it became intertwined with religion from Prague to Tbilisi. It was not that the communist parties neglected ethnicity. Whatever their internationalist pretensions, and all the talk about the international working class, they promoted the crudest chauvinism. The problem was simply that a vast empire cannot support every nationalism at once, without inviting self-destruction, whereas religion can. Religion is as serviceable for the German Silesian minority as for the Polish majority. Local nationalisms are unwilling to be compliant vehicles of domination from the centre, whether that centre be Moscow or Belgrade.

The power elites of communism could harness nationalism in only two situations: the nationalism of the centre and the nationalism of certain groups in some of the extreme peripheries. Consider first the nationalism of the centre, for example, Russian nationalism, Serbian nationalism, and, in a somewhat different context, Romanian nationalism. This nationalism at the centre involves the conscious deployment of churches under strict control as vehicles of national sentiment. In the Russian case it also involved the use of the Russian Orthodox Church against the autocephalous churches of the Ukraine and the proscribed Uniate Church of the western Ukraine, regarded as reservoirs of Ukrainian nationalism. This religious imperialism was pursued with great seriousness, and was one reason why in 1988 the millennium was primarily celebrated in Moscow rather than in Kiev. Similar considerations affected relations between the Belgrade government and the Serbian Orthodox Church, especially after Tito; and the mingling of nationalist and religious motifs increased as Albanian Muslims put pressure on the sacred and historic Serbian shrine at Kosovo. Again, in Romania, Ceausescu utilised the Orthodox Church, both as a bastion of Romanian distinctiveness, and as a weapon against extensive ethnic minorities and their distinctive religious traditions. It is, perhaps, no wonder the Romanian revolution began in the resistance offered by a Hungarian Calvinist pastor. It also underlines why the Patriarch offered, or was forced to offer, his support to Ceausescu up to the last moments before his downfall.

The other semi-viable link between the communist power elites at the centre and a mingling of religion and ethnicity is where a nation at the periphery of the empire is exposed to more pressing and proximate local enemies. That has been the case either historically or quite recently in Bulgaria vis-á-vis the Turks and in Armenia vis-á-vis the Turks and the Azeris. The situation resembles the British relationship to Sikhs threatened by Indian Hindu oppression and to Karens threatened by Burmese Buddhist oppression.

This introduces another element visible once an imperial power goes into decline: the oppression exercised by the oppressed against their own minorities, and the transfer of the rhetoric of persecution from group to group. Religion becomes a badge of identity in internecine feuds pursued down to the level of a village or part of a village or a suburb. Examples are legion: current murders in small Bosnian towns and across demarcations in Serbo-Croat villages. Armenian Christians will press against local Azeri Muslim minorities in Nagorny Karabakh, Azeris against the enclave of Nagorny Karabakh and Armenian suburbs of Baku. Protestants in Londonderry will press against what is a local Catholic majority, while being themselves a majority in the province, a minority in Ireland, a majority in the British Isles, and a minority in Europe. In the current dispute in Tatarstan over autonomy between indigenous Russians and indigenous Muslim Tatars, the Muslims tore down the Russian cross, since they identified Muscovite rule with Christianity. It is the same logic as threw down the statue of Lenin in Tashkent and replaced it by Tamerlane the Great, and it pursues its course irrespective of the presence of the badge of religion. It is a property of bonding as such. Thus in Bulgaria, the Bulgarian communists oppressed or effectively expelled the Turks and the Bulgarian Muslims. Everything is referred back to the primal deed of who originally murdered whom. Everyone looks for a potential ally against the pre-eminent threat of the moment, whomever that may be, and in local imbroglios of this kind each group finds proxies in larger perhaps more distant powers who are often of the same religious persuasion, but sometimes not, depending on geopolitical advantage. Countries can become cockpits of proxies as they relate to religion and to other markers.

The geopolitical dynamics are often at their most illuminating when they relate to three or four-cornered disputes, and where the placing of frontiers determines who is minority and who a majority. In Moldova, for example, the Gagauz, who are a Turkish speaking Christian group could find themselves allied with the forces of the Russian minority of the 'Dnieper Republic' in the east of the country. They would both of them be allied against a Romanian majority which has recently freed itself from Russian domination and may seek affiliation with Romania. In this imbroglio, Cossacks actually declared themselves partisans of 'holy Russia'.

In Bosnia-Herzegovina the largest single group in the area, over 40%, consists of Bosnian converts to Islam, but they are allied temporarily with the Catholic Croats, who are under 20%, against the Orthodox Serbs, who are not only the second largest minority at above 30% but the largest single group in the whole of what was the Yugoslav federation.

Of course, there are religious protests against the powerful pull of ethnic and geopolitical dynamics: in Serbia a huge though confused crowd gathered in front of the new cathedral in protest against the war and governmental brutality; in Lithuania priests have protested against the identification of religion with national interests; religious leaders in the Russian minorities in the Baltic states have appealed to Russians to act as good citizens, not as partisans of mother Russia. Church leaders have often tried to act similarly in Northern Ireland. Such efforts are not likely to succeed. The mixing of populations, at a particular stage in the development of national consciousness, leads to reinforcements of the markers of identity, including religion, and to mutual repulsion. Prior to that stage mixed populations seem able to coexist, at least intermittently, even in places like the Lebanon and Albania: after that stage there begins an exchange of populations and the homogenisation both of the national and religious groups. The Muslims leave Crete and Bulgaria; the Orthodox Greeks leave Turkey and northern Cyprus. Middle Eastern Christians migrate all over the world.

What we are seeing is a seismic adjustment which cancels the older pluralism of adjacent communities and thrusts out large historic groups from ancient habitats to join with people of their own nation and/or religion across the main frontier. In part this process occurs because empires collapse and the ethnic representatives of the ex-imperial power are left exposed, for example, Russians in all the non-Russian Republics. In part it is a continuation of a process of homogenisation which began with Spain in 1492, but continued, for example, in Ireland and Turkey in 1922 and is clearly operative throughout the whole of the contemporary Muslim world. The tension increases as you come to the frontiers of the great world confessions, in Cyprus or Thrace or Ossetia or Abkazia or Fermanagh. The intimacies of life in these places are astonishingly similar and yet the great confessions constitute worlds of genuine difference. They are the great codes regulating vast civilisations.

After all, religion is not only bound in with intimacies and with ethnic identities but also has reference points across the conventional frontiers. Indeed, religion is one reason why older maps exist like older paintings underneath contemporary configurations. The older map is there beneath the imperial or central overprinting and is reactivated. The Croats and Slovenes belong to a central and Catholic Europe and the moment the centre weakened they reverted. The women lit the candles in the churches and the men went to the barricades. These historic recollections have remade Europe since 1989 and are capable of reviving all kinds of ancient alliances, and of shifting whole nations into different cultural areas.

It is, and has been, of crucial importance, that Poland, Lithuania and the western Ukraine have looked to the Vatican and the West. The Estonians find themselves rejoining Lutheran Scandinavia. The Armenians and Azeris are pulled into the Middle Eastern vortex; Turkey and Iran struggle for religious and political influence in the Central Asian republics. And all along the frontiers people on the wrong side of the fence recollect their ancient affiliations, sustained by religious rituals and liturgical languages as well as by the other markers of identity and ethnicity; for example, the scattered German, Polish, Hungarian, Albanian and Greek communities of eastern Europe. Or else the religious frontier re-emerges as a crucial one, as in time it will between Czech lands and Catholic Slovakia, even though most Slovakians are at the moment opposed to independence. A large number of political parties then emerge combining religious affiliations and nationalistic roots, like the Christian Democrats of Slovakia. Often these parties are quite small, as in Serbia, but they are the visible surface of large subterranean forces. The very existence of a St. Saba party in Serbia is a portent.

The way in which the great codes, above all Islam and Christianity interact with the intimacies of life at the confused confessional frontiers, and there define worlds of difference, reminds us that religion is currently providing one of the major markers of what *is* Europe. We in north western Europe may not know it, in part because our cultural frontier is the ocean, and we can afford our historical amnesia, but Turks and Greeks know it, and so do the Russians and Kazakhs. The culturally viable Europe which is 'our common European home' thins out eastward according to a complex set of criteria: the diminution in capitalist prosperity, the lack of long-term independence and liberal experience, and crucially the presence of the Byzantines, the Ottomans and Islam. Things alter sharply as you cross the frontiers that constitute experience of Byzantine and Ottoman domination, or both together, or in succession, and mere fissures become chasms as you move from Christianity to Islam. Going south and east you pass into the Serbian enclaves of Croatia, like Knin, then into the enclaves of Islam in Bosnia and Bulgaria, until finally you reach the outer limits of Europe in Nagorny Karabakh and the thinning out of the extensive Russian populations of Kazakhstan. The ambiguity of Turkey, from the European viewpoint, is essentially its Islamic inheritance and the visible growth of militant Islamic religiosity against the partial westernisation pursued by Ataturk.

The upshot of all these changes in eastern Europe has been a vast, and given the possibilities and precedents, an amazingly peaceable shift towards older maps. St. Petersburg marks a shift away from communism to a Christian history and an eighteenth century civilisation. Karl Marx Stadt and Stalingrad, like Leningrad are no more; the great parades of imperial communist power fade away; the ikons of Lenin are brought down; and the mausolea and museums of atheism are closed or are closing. The flags of ancient territories and peoples replace the hammer and sickle. On the other side of the coin, President Yeltsin attends the high points of the Orthodox liturgical year; the cathedrals of St. Petersburg, Moscow, Kiev, Vilnius and Lvov return to their rightful owners, Orthodox, Uniate or Catholic. In Timisoara, near where the Romanian revolution began, the state has decreed a memorial to the martyrs of the revolution, close by the cathedral. Their death is to be annually celebrated in conjunction with the Feast of the Ascension.

Nor is the shift merely symbolic, if anything can be described as merely symbolic. It attests a vast reversal which as recently as 1988 Patrick Michel said could occur only 'by some miracle' (Michel 1991:125ff). The relationship of Polish Catholicism to Solidarity was exemplary. The outward and visible signs were the vast pilgrimages, above all to Czestochowa. And, as Timothy Garton Ash has argued, Poland's resistance was crucial to what occurred in the late eighties. Economic failure, massive pollution, the denial of basic human and political rights, the ripple effects of perestroika, and Gorbachev's refusal to send in the tanks, all played a part, but religion positioned the avalanche.

Even in the toughest redoubts, the role of religion was clearly visible. And people knew what they did. Romanian television announced the death of Ceausescu on December 25th with the words 'The tyrant dies on Christmas Day'. In northern Albania large crowds gathered spontaneously on All Souls Day, 1990, and turned the first public baptism for twenty-five years into the first public eucharist. In the western Ukraine the banners among the early demonstrators showed how the nationalist movement 'Rukh' drew on roots in Uniate Catholicism. In Sofia priests moved about in vans among the protesting crowds, celebrating the eucharist and baptising hundreds, while people conducted dramatic rites of purification and students set up a City of Truth adjacent to the Church of St. George. Dimitrov was silently removed from his mausoleum by night. In Tbilisi, Georgia the crowds which in early 1989 danced and prayed all night in the main square, chanted 'For God, for Georgia, for independence'. Even if one wants to question this eminent role of religion in these changes, it is interesting to observe that the Chinese government followed up Tiananmen Square with immediate repressive measures against the Christian churches. President Weizäcker did not go to the Church of Reconciliation in Berlin after the collapse of the wall, or President Havel into St. Vitus' Cathedral to acknowledge a mere epiphenomenon of economic hardship. To offer such an analysis is to indicate just how far the residual refuge of Marxism and, above all, of its background assumptions, is the western intelligentsia.

These extraordinary reversals: the attenuation of political dogma, the eminent role of religion in the peaceful revolutions of 1989–90, the emergence of a new Europe, the cantonisation of the continent from Aberystwyth to Moldova, add their weight of the unexpected and unpredicted to the world-wide rise of conservative evangelical Christianity and militant Islam. They have deconstructed our taken for granted world and to my mind they necessitate *inter alia* a thorough going reconstruction of the subject of sociology.

2

European Cultural Identity and Religion
Richard Roberts

The construction of a European cultural identity in an ever more closely integrated continent is not simply a matter of observing and quantifying patterns of individual or collective choice made in a postmodern 'market-place' of ethnic and religious identities embedded in residual local traditions. Within a re-enlarged Europe, ancestral ethnic and localised cultural identities are in a state of resurgence; and, besides this, an active 'market' in imported religiosities has opened up in Eastern Europe where governments have been seeking to establish free markets in the context of total, or near total economic collapse. There now takes place active bidding on the ideological level for the allegiance of populations emerging from Marxist-Leninist 'pseudo-modernity' (Ivan Varga).[1] The collapse of European metanarratives (Lyotard 1989) in the former Western Europe would appear to contrast markedly with the intense competition in the East between different cultural forces (often with strong religious components) which are vying with each other for hegemony in the normative vacuum created by the demise of Marxist-Leninist socialism. Across both contexts the now near universal and virtually unchallenged 'hegemon' of transnational capitalism (Sklair 1991) seeks to impose a globalised consumer culture.

---

1. Communication at the SISR Conference, Maynooth, August 1991.

The very word 'Europeanisation' in this contemporary context is thus a deeply ambiguous term. The latter may be understood in the context of the 'New Europe' and the European Community as the process by which a configuration of nation states cede cultural identity and hegemony to a greater whole to the extent required by political and economic integration. This is a process which can be clarified through the insights of European integration studies (Salmon 1990) and globalisation theory (Robertson 1991, Featherstone 1990). 'Europeanisation' also, however, implies an uneasy confrontation with the 'old Europe'. It is important to explore how this 'old' European identity (and its variations) emerged, differentiated itself, enjoyed a near global triumph, and then 'declined'. Religious and theological elements have been of central importance (both positive and negative) in the transformations of the 'idea' and identity of the 'old' Europe.

In the contemporary context, complex tensions now arise between the modernising conformity required by multi-national capitalism and its concomitant European integration and its 'Europe' on the one hand, and, on the other, the 'old' Europe of nationalisms, ethnic diversity, anti-Semitism, fear of Islam, and the renewed Roman Catholic ideology of 'Christendom' on the other. There thus now exists the uneasy juxtaposition of pre-modern traditions, aspects of radical modernity, and post-modern factors in a complex problematic, some aspects of which are clarified below.

The origins of the idea of Europe are shrouded in myth (see Hubner 1985 for a wide-ranging account of theories of myth). In the time of Homer the name 'Europe' applied to Middle Greece. Gradually the designation spread to the whole Greek mainland and then in the colonisation period it came to refer to one of the three great journey directions away from the homeland (the others being Asia and Libya). In the later Greek and then the Roman period the sense of a known mainland extended north and west. The historical evolution of Europe prior to the Christian era was profoundly influenced by migrations of Indogermanic peoples and population movements.

Awareness of the extreme complexity of the task of isolating European identity is not new. Systems of management of this complexity may be organised under the two interconnected headings of periodisation and the differentiation of traditions (or 'narratives') respectively. Traditions can be understood as competing 'meta-narratives' that each seek to appropriate authority and sometimes hegemonic status as bearers of authentic European identity. It will become apparent that neither 'epochs' nor 'narratives' as traditionally conceived and exploited can answer the legitimate demands of a satisfactory sociological account of the contemporary definition of Europe and European identities. In short, comprehension of the transitions from the 'old' to the 'new' Europes will require a conceptual shift from narrative and historical understanding of traditions (and stages in their evolution) to a theoretical explanation of the contemporary co-existence of pre-modern, modern and postmodern cultural factors.

Periodisation and Traditions

The English Roman Catholic historian and commentator on the idea of Europe Christopher Dawson (1932, 1948, 1952), argued for a seven stage account of the history of Western culture.[2] Dawson's viewpoint was eurocentric in the extreme: 'The existence of Europe is the basis of the historical development of the modern world, and it is only in relation to that fact that the development of each particular state can be understood' (1952:24). Nevertheless, in historical terms, Dawson recognised that the growing consciousness of nationality and of the nation-state had tended to leave 'Europe in the background as a vague abstraction or as nothing more than a geographical expression' (*ibid.*). In addition, he maintained that the conception of Europe never held a definite place in a tradition of education that was dominated by the history of the ancient world of Greece and Rome, and, at a much lower level, by consciousness of an individual's own country. Dawson thus concluded shortly after the Second World War, 'To ignore Europe and to concentrate all our attention on the political community to which we belong, as though it was the whole social reality, leads in the last resort to the totalitarian state, and National Socialism itself was only this development carried out with Germanic thoroughness and Prussian ruthlessness' (1952:25).

Dawson developed a distinctive standpoint which places him thoroughly in the 'Christendom' tradition (Aretin 1970, Belloc 1962, Hanson 1987, Kees 1960, Lortz 1959, Novak 1989, Schwartz 1980). Europe as such is defined as 'a

---

2. See also Troeltsch 1922 who reviews the periodisations offered by Hegel, Ranke, Guizot, Harnack, Weber and Sombart, amongst others.

community of peoples who share in a common spiritual tradition that had its origins three thousand years ago in the eastern Mediterranean and which has been transmitted from age to age and from people to people until it has come to overshadow the world' (Dawson 1952:26). For Dawson, Europe could only be understood by the study of Christian culture, for 'it was as Christendom that Europe first became conscious of itself as a society of peoples with common moral values and common spiritual aims' (1952:26).

The Roman Catholic Church has traditionally invested heavily in the conception of a Christian Europe and this idea has undergone systematic renovation during the pontificate of Pope John Paul II. An important and unambiguous expression of papal convictions is to be found in two important statements 'Cyril and Methodius' (1980) and 'Europe and the Faith' (1985). In the earlier document Pope John Paul laid down the theological ground rules for a historic decade during which several important anniversaries of the millennium of the conversion of Eastern Europe would take place (e.g. Poland 986; Hungary 982; the Rus of Kiev 988). Thus in 'Cyril and Methodius' John Paul II made a strategic ideological pre-emptive strike by bringing together the patronage of Western Europe by St Benedict declared by Paul VI in 1964 with his own declaration of the patronage of Eastern Europe by the Thessalonican brothers Cyril (d. 869) and Methodius (d. 885). Subsequent developments have indicated the wisdom of this commitment (as seen from the standpoint of the Roman Catholic Church), now that inter-denominational struggles (suppressed by Marxism-Leninism) have once more broken out after the collapse of communism in 1989-90.

For Pope John Paul II: 'Europe, in fact, as a geographical whole, is, so to speak, the fruit of two currents of Christian traditions, to which are added also two different, but at the same time deeply complementary, forms of culture' (John Paul II 1980:17). The proclamation of the co-patronage of Cyril and Methodius combines historical justification with the future reference of the 'signs of the times' as a sanctification and legitimation of the present. Thus the new-born Europe of the Dark Ages 'ensured the Europe of today a common spiritual and cultural heritage' (1980:18). The second Apostolic Letter, 'Europe and the Faith' is a document that contains a far fuller account of the papal understanding of contemporary Europe and the relevance to it of its 'Christian roots' than the earlier Letter. John Paul II begins with a characterisation of the contemporary Europe whose destiny is now at stake:

> The Europe to which we are sent out has undergone such cultural, political, social and economic transformations as to formulate the problem of evangelisation in totally new terms. We could even say that Europe, as she has appeared following the complex events of the last century, has presented Christianity and the Church with the most radical challenge history has witnessed, but at the same time opened the way today to new and creative possibilities for the proclamation and incarnation of the Gospel. (1985:279)

Christendom as a conception has always existed most powerfully in the reconstructive imagination of those who propound its virtues; and it is precisely the tendency to construct such an all-embracing transnational cultural identity which has created enormous historic problems. The defence of Christendom has from the time of Augustine involved the enforcement and employment of sanctions as the means of sustaining its integrity. Thus the Crusades ostensibly directed at the recovery of the Holy City were matched by internal campaigns which, as in the case of the Albigenses, were directed at the elimination of dissent within Christian Europe.

Europe: the Politics of Representation

Two important areas of concern stand out with regard to the definition and defence of the identity of Christendom.[3] The first is the treatment of the Jews; the second is the relationship with Islam. The distinguished Palestinian (but Christian Arab originating) critic Edward Said (1978) has explored the representation of the East and Islam through the academic discipline of 'Orientalism'. Here we encounter the cultural construction of a reality outside and over against that of Christianity and Christendom. This process, conducted in conjunction with the emergent scientific study of cultures in the late eighteenth century onwards which

---

3. For introduction to the background see: Castles, Booth and Wallace (1984), Cecchini (1988), Daniel (1975), Edwards (1988), Herrin (1987), Lehmann (1984), Watt (1972), Wright (1982).

had at its very centre the construction of discourses of representation, is an activity now justifiably regarded as involving the 'politics of representation'. Edward Said begins by designating the Orient and its special place in European experience in the following way:

> The Orient is not only adjacent to Europe; it is also the place of Europe's greatest and richest and oldest colonies, the source of its civilisations and languages, its cultural contestant, and one of its deepest and most recurrent images of the Other. In addition, the Orient has helped to define Europe (or the West) as its contrasting image, idea, personality, experience. (Said 1978:1–2)

Said's designation of the Orient as 'the Other' reflects Hegelian influence and indeed the dialectics of lordship and bondage. According to Said, Orientalism as an allegedly scientific study is understood by Muslims as 'a Western strategy for dominating, restructuring, and having authority over the Orient' (1978:3). Thus the representation and interpretation of Islam within the ambit of Orientalism is the exercise of a form of cultural hegemony (in Gramsci's understanding of the term). This impinges directly upon the major concerns of this chapter, for, Said argues:

> Orientalism is never far from what Denys Hay has called the idea of Europe, a collective notion identifying 'us' Europeans as against all 'those' non-Europeans, and indeed it can be argued that the major components in European culture is precisely what made that culture hegemonic both in and outside Europe: the idea of European identity as a superior one in comparison with all non-European peoples and cultures (1978:7).

The historian Henri Pirenne has argued that the Islamic invasions beginning in the seventh century served to shift the centre of European culture northwards away from the Mediterranean and into a form of enclosure: the Romano-German civilisation of the Holy Roman Empire. Christendom thus became the 'one great Christian community, conterminous with the ecclesia.... The Occident was now living its own life' (1939:234, 283).

Said's argument concerning Orientalism is relevant to our understanding of the cultural politics affecting the representation of Europe itself. It was in the context of the Enlightenment, in particular that side of the German Enlightenment imbued with Romanticism, that the construction of the Oriental and Islamic 'other' took place in the same intellectual and social context in which the discussion of the relationship of modernity with Protestant Europe began. Here the tensions between the inner-European struggle for cultural hegemony (exemplified supremely by the nineteenth century conflict between France and Germany), industrialisation, the formation of modern disciplines in the humanities, and imperialism (both political and cultural) converged within a context characterised by the rapid and pervasive secularisation of culture. With the general loss of confidence in the Biblical texts and the Christian metanarrative as the cultural underpinning of the cultural hegemony expressed in the conception of Christendom, the Romantics and their associates turned eastwards. They transplanted the Christian motif of dying and rising to a renascent Orient, an Indo-European well-spring of culture exposed by means of philology, which could serve in turn as the means of regenerating a Europe deprived of its Christian myth/history (Said 1978:115). Modern orientalism is thus seen to derive both from secularising factors and the Romantic remythologisation of culture in late eighteenth century European thought (1978:120). These are the sources of the dynamics of mythopoiesis.

In short, according to Said, 'the Orientalist could celebrate his method, his position, as that of a secular creator, a man who made new worlds as God had once made the old' (1978:121). In terms of the leitmotif of nineteenth century scholarship and intellectual life, the ideal had indeed displaced the real. These possibilities of displacement have now become actualities for those possessing sufficient cultural capital to re-create themselves in postmodernity.

Protestantism, Modernity and Europe

Ernst Troeltsch (1912) wrote *Protestantism and Progress* at the high point of European self-confidence (*see* Mehl 1959, Pfeffer 1957, Roser 1979, Walz 1955). In 1912, the Western world stood at the brink of one of the most destructive wars of human history. Not only this, but he touched upon issues that impinge upon the deepest currents of the German contribution to the identity of Europe. Troeltsch sought to gain insight into the intellectual and religious situation of his day 'from which the significance and the possibilities of development possessed by Christianity might be deduced' (1912:v–vi) and it was this that led him to:

> engage in historical investigations regarding the spirit of the modern world, for this can only be understood in the light of its relation to the earlier epochs of Christian civilisation in Europe. As Adolf Harnack has described the genesis and disintegration of Christian dogma, so I should like to examine the present situation and its significance for the fate of Christianity in the modern world. (1912:vi)

Troeltsch held that 'the living possibilities of development and progress are to be found on Protestant soil' (1912:vii–viii) and not in an archaic Catholicism. It was this anticipation which governed his priorities, which were to be pursued in strictly historical terms, purportedly without theological bias. Despite his desire for objectivity, Troeltsch nevertheless sought to distinguish the perennially valuable elements in modern civilisation from the transient and he tried to establish a position of stable compromise, that is

> to give the religious ideas of Christianity – which I hold to be the sole really religious force in our European system of civilisation, and which I also believe to be superior to the religions of the East – a shape and form capable of doing justice to the absoluteness of religious conviction, and at the same time in harmony with the valuable elements in the modern spirit. (Troeltsch 1912:85–6)

Troeltsch proceeded to expound the ambiguous role of Protestantism in the history of Western Europe and North America. Protestantism first appeared as a 'revival and reinforcement of the ideal of authoritatively imposed Church-civilisation' which served to revive the catholic idea and relaunched the 'medieval spirit' for a further two centuries. It was only in the late seventeenth and the eighteenth centuries that the struggle for freedom took place which effectively terminated the middle ages and launched Protestantism as a vehicle of modernity.

The Negation of 'Europe'

Whereas traditional Catholicism has retained its commitment to the idea of Christendom and (liberal) Protestantism opted for an alliance with modernity (and Said exposes the cultural politics of both) the real precursor of the contemporary dilemmas concerning the idea of Europe is the German cultural critic and historian Oswald Spengler (1880–1939; see Hughes 1952, Dray 1980) whose long-neglected book *The Decline of the West* (1918)[4] offers a distinctly contemporary challenge, inasmuch as he propounds a ruthless cultural relativism activated by the naked ontological assertion of the striving self.

Spengler in typical German fashion (and like Heidegger later in the century) relates the most fundamental and general levels of discourse together: 'The decline of the West ... we now perceive to be a philosophical problem that, when comprehended in all its gravity, includes within itself every great question of Being' (1926:3). Spengler's thematic moves from the present-day into a

> new philosophy – the philosophy of the future, so far as the metaphysically-exhausted soil of the west can bear such, and in any case the only philosophy which is within the *possibilities* of the West European mind in its next stages. It expands into the conception of a *morphology of world history*, of the world as history in contrast to the morphology of the world-as-nature that hitherto has been almost the only theme of philosophy. (1926:5)

All branches of a culture are bound together in the 'morphological relationship', that is in a logic not only of time (which explains the 'organic necessity' in life - Destiny) but also what Spengler calls the 'logic of space' (1926:6–7). 'Man' is a meaning-forming conscious organism faced with an ongoing problem of the

---

4. He extended his ideas in Spengler (1931), translated in 1932.

scale of effort required to secure 'world-formation'; in other words he/she is now postmodern.

Spengler dismisses the traditional subdivision of history into Ancient, Medieval and Modern. These are terms which distort the immensity of world history as the history of many cultures. The very word Europe comes in for pointed attack. Spengler stresses the constructed and transient character of all characterisations of Europe, indeed:

> The word 'Europe' ought to be struck out of history. There is historically no 'European' type, and it is sheer delusion to speak of the Hellenes as 'European Antiquity'.... It is thanks to the word 'Europe' alone, and the complex of ideas resulting from it, that our historical consciousness has come to link Russia with the West in an utterly baseless unity.... 'East' and 'West' are notions that contain real history, whereas 'Europe' is an empty sound. (1926:16)

Spengler's historical Copernican revolution involves a radical de-centring of the European subject and its conceits. In this 'Civilisation', it is money that comes to the fore as dominant cultural phenomenon and, for Spengler, Cecil Rhodes was its emblematic hero. This is a form of deconstruction *avant la lettre*, and, moreover, it presages a fluid, and yet more radical postmodernity of the kind envisaged by Jean-François Lyotard as

> incredulity towards metanarratives. This incredulity is undoubtedly a product of progress in the sciences: but that progress in turn presupposes it. To the obsolescence of the metanarrative apparatus of legitimation corresponds, most notably, the crisis of metaphysical philosophy and of the university institution which in the past relied on it. The narrative function is losing its functors, its great hero, its great dangers, its great voyages, its great goal. It is being dispersed in clouds of language narrative elements – narrative, but also denotative, prescriptive, descriptive, and so on. Conveyed within each cloud are pragmatic valencies specific to its kind. Each of us lives at the intersection of many of these. However, we do not necessarily establish stable language combinations, and the properties of the ones we do establish are not necessarily communicable. (1979:14)

Shortly after the Second World War (and the second defeat of Germany), Karl Löwith (1949) was to assert in *Meaning and History* that Western thought consisted in a quasi-theodicic struggle between Christ and Prometheus, that is between a Christian culture (however vestigial as a result of secularisation) as opposed to the culture of self-aggrandisement. For Spengler, the latter had triumphed in the Faustian soul of a culture and mentality which celebrates expansive power in all spheres of human endeavour, despite any unfortunate world-historical outcomes. The inevitable descent into hell took place. In our own time, Francis Fukuyama, a latter-day Spengler, propounds the 'end of history' and drives further forward analogous prognostications.

The New Europe

It is now apparent that the definition of Europe and of a European identity involves a struggle for, as it were, the very soul of Europe. The historical and societal context of the re-emergence of Eastern Europe into the mainstream is very complex.[5] Many factors have to be taken into account which cannot be explored here. In this connection it is, however, worth noting that Mikhail Gorbachev propounded an inherently optimistic vision of Europe which shares much with that of the papacy, yet his account is crucially different. In contrast to Spengler, Gorbachev maintains that

> Europe 'from the Atlantic to the Urals' is a cultural-historical entity united by the common heritage of the Renaissance and the Enlightenment, of the great philosophical and social teachings of the nineteenth and twentieth centuries. These are powerful magnets which help policy-makers in their search for ways to mutual understanding and cooperation at the level of interstate relations. A tremendous potential for a policy of peace and neighbourliness is inherent in the European cultural heritage. Generally, in Europe the new, salutary outlook knows much more fertile ground than in any other region where the two regions come into contact (Gorbachev 1987:198).

---

5. Aganbegyan (1988), Ash (1989), Ash (1990), Dahrendorf (1990), Dawisha (1988), Gorbachev, (1988), Lane (1990), Michel (1991), Ramet (1989).

The removal of the Iron Curtain would appear to imply a series of reversions in European identity – but to which image or images? The consolidation of the European Community has involved the construction of a modern Europe based on the Franco-German axis (virtually a secularised version of the tradition of Charlemagne based on the Rhine Corridor). Contrary to this, the Roman Catholic and papal vision is *not* focused on the Rhine (and thus on the reconciliation of a revolutionary and Catholic France with a prosperous and primarily Protestant Germany) but on a Greater Europe *including* Russia and the Ukraine. Hence this explains the East–West emphasis in the papal Letters and the exclusion of the Protestant/Catholic split from consideration.

The United Kingdom stands irresolutely at the periphery having participated in twentieth century history as patient rather than agent. There has been no ideological definition of Europeanness as such at British government policy level; in fact the policy is not to allow such an identity to develop. Argument has been pursued almost exclusively at the level of the extension and integration of markets. As Miriam Camps has argued in a judgment that retains validity, 'there has never been much real understanding in the United Kingdom of the depth of the drive towards real unity, as distinct from intergovernmental cooperation, on the continent' (1964:339).

The 'New Europe' which has evolved since the Second World War was created in order to resolve a historic problem. As Nicoll and Salmon point out:

> Throughout history, the European continent has been restless, fragile and contradictory, competitive and pluralist. Responding unlike the subjects of the Chinese, Javanese and Ottoman Empires, to no central rule-making authority, and divided from each other by language and religion, and by princely, and later national aspirations, the Europeans vied with each other and stimulated to create a civilisation, proprietorially described simply as 'civilisation', which it became their manifest destiny to spread across the planet. (1990:1)

Despite the common strands of Christianity, the Graeco-Roman heritage of philosophy and law, the humanism of the Renaissance, and, much later, the principles of representative democracy, Western Europeans were 'more or less in constant strife with each other in the four centuries up to the middle of the twentieth' (*ibid.*). Two crucial factors seem to have provoked the emergence of the New Europe: first, the conviction that the European conflicts of the twentieth century had to be stopped; second, a realisation that after the Second World War mainland Europe was no longer a true world power in the face of the USSR and the United States.

Nicoll and Salmon trace the idea of the New Europe back to such sources as the apocryphal 'Grand Design' of Henry IV (1553–1610) of France, to William Penn (1644–1718) and his essay of 1693, Immanuel Kant's (1724–1804) treatise of 1795, 'Zum ewigen Frieden', Saint-Simon (1760–1825) and Augustin Thierry's 'On the Reorganisation of European Society' (1814) and Carlo Cattaneo's (1801–1869) idea of subsidiarity.

The First World War confirmed the crisis of the nation-state and the need for new thinking. Thus Richard Coudenhove-Kalergi founded the Pan-European movement in 1923 and produced the 'Pan-European manifesto' in 1924 and Aristide Briand outlined a plan for European Union in the 10th General Assembly of the League of Nations on 7 September 1929 which was elaborated by the French Government into 'The Organisation of a Regime of European Federal Union' presented to the League in May 1930.

In all of this, however, the actual question of the cultural identity of Europe has been a peripheral issue. It is precisely the problematic historic identities of Europe which have made the pragmatic transnationalism of the processes of European integration so important. It is precisely at the point at which the post-war questions of unity in policy as opposed to the mere cooperation between states come to the fore that the ancestral problems of identity re-emerge. Progress in the 1970s was slow because of a reluctance to address the gap between the rhetoric about European identity and European union and measures required to effect fundamental change. The 'European Identity' document published in Copenhagen in 1973 (European Community 1973) spoke of a definition of identity but little was done. The Single European Act of 1985 speaks of 'a European identity in external policy matters', but even this has proved a conception difficult to realise.

The political impetus which gave rise to the post-war drive towards cooperation and the idea of a united Europe expressed in the Treaty of Rome as 'an ever closer union among the peoples of Europe' has foundered on the problem of the definition of goals. As Nicolls and Salmon comment: 'The European destination is still unknown' (1990:229). The ideas of Sully, Penn, Saint-Simon and Cattaeno 'have been transformed into living institutions and systems' (232) and yet a distinctive theological vision of Europe has not been readily assimilable into the complex mixture of ideals and prudential pragmatism characteristic of the emergence of the new Europe. Nicolls and Salmon conclude with the following remark: 'The very word "community" is symbolic of the nature of the endeavour. European construction is not solely about economic transactions or a single integrated market but about the future nature of the political relations between states and peoples' (1990:241). Here there would appear, *a priori*, to be an obvious point of leverage for an integrative vision which would not, however, be unproblematic given the complex historical antecedents.

Conclusion: theorising the identity of Europe

A possible key to the unlocking of this overall problematic lies in the theory of globalisation as it might be applied and developed in the context of 'Europeanisation'. The application of globalisation theory to the study of the religious socio-cultural dimension has been pioneered by the sociologist Roland Robertson. Robertson is concerned to resist the comprehensive acceptance of secularisation as the marginalisation and sequestration of religion in the face of modernity. Thus sociologists of religion have declined to 'reconstruct their subdisciplinary foci' (1991:208) and have in the process become the victims of their own theory.

Robertson traces the origins of the study of 'the world' from its origins, first in international relations and then in comparative sociology: 'Comparative sociology was concerned with analytical relationships between and among societies, international relations as a discipline with concrete relationships between and among nations' (209). The emergence of Third World studies led to a profound shift in sociological thinking: 'Until our day, human society has never existed' for earlier cultures, societies and empires were bounded and 'Human culture existed "in itself", but not "for men". Human society only came to exist subjectively, men only acquired the knowledge that they were part of a single social world through the midwifery of European imperialism' (Worsley 1964:10). This analysis confirms our earlier approach to Said's *Orientalism* which itself illustrates a parallel critical inside/outside approach to cultural hegemony.

The tendency within sociology of religion in its encounter with the Third World was to extend Weber's Protestant Ethic thesis and the secularisation paradigm to this new context. The later development of dependency theory and arguments about the relative merits of development confirmed the trend of dealing with the 'world system'. Immanuel Wallerstein's extension of the idea of a *world* system does not, according to Robertson, in and of itself provide an adequate model for understanding the dynamics of the emergent *global* system. World system theory tends to subordinate cultural (and particularly religious) factors by ascribing to them merely epiphenomenal status. Robertson, following Gluck (1985), argues that such factors have a far more substantive role. Thus modernity and modernisation acquire 'mythical' status as 'the symbolic significance of modernisation as a *form* of purposive change – rather than as contentful change along objectively ascertained trajectories' (Robertson 1991:211). In such circumstances tradition had to be 'invented' (Hobsbawm and Ranger 1983) in order to meet the practical onset and mythopoeic power of modernisation. Thus, for example, 'Japan largely acquired *the idea of the need for a national identity* within the context of inter- and transnational discourse about what it meant to be a national society in an increasingly interdependent world (i.e. a world which has *by now* become a single place)' (Robertson 1991:212). Writing of the period between 1870 and 1914 Eric Hobsbawm has argued that nationalism became a new secular, surrogate religion. In this setting 'tradition was invoked – and often invented – as a condition of participation in a rapidly expanding – but yet also imploding world order' (*ibid.*).

The development of national-civil religion in the same period and the role of national elites in its creation suggests to Robertson a substantial modification and enlargement of the 'world-system' approach which tends not to admit the creative paradoxes outlined earlier. Such theory is 'thin', that is narrow in its perspective and reductive in its implications. It remains wedded to the understanding of the world as international rather than truly global. Robertson proposes a 'thicker' description embodied in the study of the global-human condition, that is a 'global-human circumstance' consisting of four basic components: '*the system of societies* (the international component); *societies*; *individuals*; and *humankind*' (215). Twentieth-century globalisation understood as a 'form of institutionalisation of world order' constitutes the problem of 'globality' (216) which has two major aspects. First, it involves 'relativisation of societal (and civilisational) cultures, individual forms of life, conceptions of the human species and of the autonomy of international relations'. In other words difference becomes a dangerous aspect of an essentially unified system. Second, globalisation 'sharpens concern with the nature, *raison d'étre* and fate of the entire world' (*ibid.*). Robertson draws the conclusion that

> the problem of globality becomes the central focus of religion in the late-twentieth century. Globalisation and the thematisation of the problem of globality as a 'dangerous' circumstance takes us beyond the problem of secularisation and yet at the same time they consolidate and extend concern with what is to be regarded as 'religious'. To be more precise, while the notion of worldliness became central to sociological thinking about religion in reference to the general problem of modernity, and in doing so created the theme of secularisation, the problem of globality (and the associated issue of postmodernity) involves the reconstruction of the concept of worldliness, the posing of new questions about the relationship between the

secular and the sacred, and considerable fluidity concerning the form and content of religion. (*ibid.*)

It is this global conception, suitably refined and newly contextualised, which might prove a suitable analytical tool in the decipherment of the current crisis in *European* identity. A thick, multi-layered and flexible mode of description and analysis is required which might be capable of coping with the dialectical juxtapositions of pre-modern traditions, aspects of modernity, and the fragmented chaos of postmodernity which is characteristic of the contemporary European condition. Such an approach would require supplementation, most probably from social psychology; but the emergence of the New Europe and the role of religion within it present important empirical and theoretical challenges to both social scientists and practitioners.

3
Religion and Democracy in Central Eastern Europe
Patrick Michel

Religion has played a significant part in the long process of emergence from communism in Central Eastern Europe. Sometimes it has played this part in the form of the Church, sometimes outside that form, and sometimes against the Church itself. The process has been one of differentiation in contrast to the homogenisation which formed the basis of the Soviet project. The simple fact of affirming that politics must be subject to ethics is itself presage of a plural mentality, because it means leaving behind totalitarianism and moving in the direction of democracy. For the churches emergence from the communist system raises the question of the type of relationship they have to develop with the new societies. This relationship can vary from one in which society is obligated to the Church to one in which a free market of values dominates. The Church has struggled for the setting up of democracy, that is, for some form of pluralism. The problem for the Church today is to define its place within this plural world. Everything seems to indicate that it will be a challenge much more difficult than that posed by the Soviet system.

I have analysed elsewhere (Michel 1992) the three types of relation between politics and religion which succeeded each other or were juxtaposed in this part of Europe during the last four decades: persecution, compromise and conflict. Here we can recall that these three types could not have developed historically in the way that they did had it not been for the status the Soviet system imposed on religion. It is due to the fact that communism refused to integrate it ideologically – and that it was the only aspect of society in this position – which gave religion the potential to be a vector for three counter-movements: the de-alienation of the individual, the de-totalisation of society and the de-sovietisation of nations. The term potential role is used because the status was just an imputed one, and it depended on the denominations and churches to seize the opportunity that it gave. But it is important to underline that it was the Soviet system itself imposing the status which placed religion in the situation of being able to play the part which it did in that area of the world. For once the system no longer exists, neither does the potential role, which must then undergo total redefinition.

Now that separate political and religious spheres have re-emerged, two basic processes have appeared: attempts to remove the 'necessary ambiguities' on which the resort to religion under communism was built, and attempts to instrumentalise religion for political gain. The second process does not require much commentary. In a situations of political instability, when all known points of reference have disappeared, it is only natural to use religion to legitimate one's management of political clientèle. One can see this in attempts in Poland, Croatia and Slovakia to mobilise Catholicism for national purposes. The religious processions in Slovakia, for example, which were undertaken to celebrate the end of communism must almost of necessity have ended up sharing in and being affected by the structuring of an evolving society. These processions witnessed to both personal and collective victories over an adversary which most of the time one had not even fought: one had taken revenge on history, tamed the past and overcome an unending chain of frustrations. But the processions also bore witness to an identity which previous experience assumed had all but disappeared, namely restoring the link with the past, a link broken by the years of communist rule, through the offices of religion – a function, one should note, which is normally the preserve of creation myths. The processions equally contributed to the reappropriation of a *national space*, by way of a sacralisation of the geography of everyday life. Their final consequence was that, in offering the chance to proclaim explicitly a Slovak identity, they allowed the possibility, rich in potential political instrumentalisations, to assume a clear (and negative) position on the union with the Czechs.[1]

The Church itself is also having to recover points of reference. To lend itself to political usage, at the risk of all its consequences (a risk which was run during the presidential campaign in Poland and during the abortion debate), indicates in the final analysis the difficulty it finds in occupying an appropriate place in the present climate of social upheaval. In Poland, and in response to the fiction of the popular will as the basis of the official communist system, there was constructed the counterfiction of a society entirely regrouped behind its Church. The disappearance of the first of these fictions leads logically today to the end of the second. The return to reality with the pluralisation of the political landscape brings to light an ambiguity which conditioned the very functioning of the mechanisms of social resistance: in opposing its own concept of totality to that which the official system imposed, the Church was earnestly defending pluralism, whether consciously or not. Various factions of society used the Church, its messages and its values emblematically, as instruments, to bring into question the legitimacy of the regime. But their choice of this vehicle which itself has totalising tendencies does not imply their adhesion to the Church's total view. In this way, Poland produced the original sociological type of the 'non-believing adherent', using religion for purposes that were explicitly non-religious. Today, in debates on human rights and on modernity, the difference between the Church on the one hand and society and the secularists on the other can be clearly seen.

Not unexpectedly, the development of such different viewpoints is related to very different conceptions of the unbending process of democracy. Even if we only look at the Polish example, we can find, in addition to the 'Western' democracy to which a Geremek or a Mazowiecki subscribe, at least two other interpretations. Cardinal Glemp has called for a 'democracy of common consent' in which, doubtlessly, Polish identity is fundamentally defined by the Catholic component. Thus, in a discourse delivered in March 1990 during a debate on the introduction of the catechism in schools, the primate affirmed,

---

1. This chapter was written before the secession of Slovakia occurred.

Close examination shows that a password for Polish identity hardly seems desirable. People do not need to give expression to it. There are those whom the term 'fatherland' irritates. It is sufficient, they say, to speak of 'country'. Why say 'nation' if we can substitute this word with 'society'? This is what they say.

On the basis of criteria presented as 'absolutes', democracy tends to become the expression of the whole people, of the nation. But referring to this totality is only an attempt to avoid establishing a vocabulary of plurality, even at the risk of nationalist exclusivity and conformity.

In fact, this reference indicates an absence of reflection by the Church on the very nature of democracy and the changes that it implies. The reintroduction of catechism in schools had not been the object of any consultation beforehand, and some of the clerics showed their aggravation when faced with negative reactions of the kind that such an introduction was bound to arouse. In this climate Bishop Goclowski of Gdansk did not hesitate to correct the question which was asked of him by a Western journalist: 'Public school? We would rather say Polish school. It is the school of a nation where 100 per cent of the children follow a religious eduction. The nation must preserve its Catholic identity, as we are taught by Polish history'. The Church has an apparent incapacity to admit the autonomy of the political, an incapacity that indicates the persistence of an attitude of control. The existence of an episcopal commission on preparations for the formation of the government is testimony enough, as is the establishment of a list of parties for which Catholics were invited to vote during the parliamentary elections. What is more, even while the episcopate was launching an appeal to the clergy, inviting them not to enter directly the political arena (for example, not to give their sermons too much of a party political tone), the episcopate came up against priests' refusal to renounce the status of 'social leaders' which had in the nature of things been held by them for some time.

The populist conception of democracy incarnated by President Walesa borrows a few themes from the idea of democracy by common consent. He calls upon these themes largely to discredit his political adversaries and consign them to that part of society that does not have thoughts befitting a 'nation'. Senator Kacynski said as much at the close of the debate on abortion in Poland: 'All good Poles are against abortion. Those who are in favour constitute the evil part of the nation'. Here, the question is naturally not that of abortion, but that of the status reserved in this case for the 'evil part of the nation'. Is that status also apt for those giving themselves the right, in the name of a truth they hold, to exclude those who do not share this truth?

In the new context of transition in which Europe and the former Iron Curtain countries find themselves today, the Catholic Church seems paradoxically at the same time reinforced and weakened. The Polish Church obtained abolition of its negative juridical status from the same communist regime which imposed it and which it had petitioned for years to remove it. From the time the communists fell from power, the Church has particularly benefited from a form of institutional influence which has continued to make it a powerful actor on the present political scene. Tadeusz Mazowiecki defines himself as a Catholic, and Lech Walesa did not cease, during the presidential campaign, to refer to religious values when treating the subject of identity. In Czechoslovakia, where the refusal to 'normalise' the Church's position was maintained until the collapse of the soviet system, the episcopal hierarchy remained below strength until the 'Velvet Revolution', despite nominations made in the last period of communist rule. The hierarchy is now reconstituted and the Church enjoys an authentic prestige. This is despite the fact that even in Bohemia religion has become a 'private affair' and clerics who had mobilised as part of the Charter movement, such as Father Vaclav Maly and Pastor Milos Rejchrt, have rejected using public law to recover their parishes.

Finally, in Hungary, where the Church has had restored to it all possessions except land previously confiscated by the communist regime, the bishops tried to get people to forget the positions they held under communism. To do so, they worked on the rehabilitation of the figure of Cardinal Mindszenty. The former cardinal primate of Hungary had been a ferocious opponent of the communist regime. The solemn transfer of his remains to Eszergom, in May 1991, permitted the Church to pose as a victim of communism. As with school text books behind the Iron Curtain, the history of the relations between Church and state in Hungary had been continually reworked and during the seventies and eighties official history deliberately overlooked the role of Mindszenty. But now it is Cardinal Lekai, his successor at the head of the Hungarian Church and creator of the politics of 'small steps', who is now forgotten.

At the same time, as we have already noted, the ambiguities that had made possible the instrumentalisation of religion for the political purpose of the struggle against the Soviet system are disappearing. The Church applied itself to helping Polish society give birth to a modern political system. Today, the Church must find its place within it. Yet all the indications are that the goal is difficult to obtain. In effect, the Church will have to abandon all pretensions to the kind of centre-stage role which was its lot during the years of resistance. As Adam Michnik once said, 'To live out pluralism is to know how to limit oneself, to know that we live with others and to make that cohabitation livable'. But limiting oneself is nothing other than leaving the sphere of totality in order to enter into that of the relative. Yet the Polish Church seems to have some difficulty in going down this path: the politics of confrontation that was so successful with the Soviet regime has scarcely prepared it for its meeting with modernity. Of course, Poland's encounter with modernity has a particular importance, because of the Polish origins of the present pope and the type of status which his Church claims in that country. In fact Polish Catholicism has benefited from the forced secularisation which a political power with a totalitarian ideology attempted to introduce. From the middle of the nineteen seventies, it seemed clear to certain people on the Polish scene that the suppression of the totalitarian political structure itself could alone bring about a laicisation of society. At the end of the nineteen eighties, the same persons had some reason to suggest that, if that exhausted structure was not liquidated, there was a risk of a religious takeover of the country on the pattern of the Iranian Revolution. Today that perspective is no longer relevant. On the contrary, the pluralisation and democratisation of Polish society might seem to be putting into place the minimal conditions of a Quebec-type scenario, namely a rapid weakening of Catholicism brought about by the rallying of Polish society around the values of American-style modernity. The victory of Stan Tymynski over Tadeusz Mazowiecki in the first round of the presidential election constituted from this point view a serious warning. In not protesting against the use of Catholicism as the constitutive criteria of Polish identity, a use made for electoral purposes by Walesa and his entourage, the Church no doubt aimed to reaffirm the central character of its position on the

Polish scene. Resting on the prestige it gained from its role in standing up to the communist power, the Church seems to be applying itself to compensate for a decrease in social influence by an increase in its institutional weight. More than the Quebec scenario, the Church fears in effect the development of the Spanish model, the ousting of the dictatorship and the passage to a democracy in which the Catholic position is weakened. It is true that a decrease in recruitment to the seminaries was of the order of ten per cent in 1990 and that priests are now in the position of having to contest their status as social leaders. We hear denouncements of the black totalitarianism that seems to have substituted itself for the red, either from the feminist associations over the 'medieval law' against abortion or more simply from the average Pole's exasperation at the enormous presence of the Church in media and education. An opinion poll in May 1991 showed that only 59 per cent of Poles were satisfied with their Church, against 83 per cent one year before; 60 per cent of those interviewed affirmed that the influence of the Church was too great.

The importance of this development is reinforced by events in the other central Eastern European countries, particularly the debates on the restitution of Church property confiscated by the communists. As noted by the Piarist Laszlo Lukacs, in Hungary during the process of restitution of all church property except land, a restitution anticipated by the law of 10 July 1991, the appeal to charity and generosity came from the political world whereas the proclamation of property rights came from the side of the Church. As noted by the pastor Milos Rejchrt, in Czechoslovakia the 'trust capital' accumulated by the Church is, as in Hungary, diminishing rapidly precisely over the issue of the restitution of church possessions. Naturally in the case of Poland, it is very difficult to predict where the relationship between the Catholic Church and Polish society will settle if one takes a scale ranging from the clericalisation of politics to the liquidation of religion's social influence. How this relationship will be defined depends on the overall recomposition of the Polish socio-political landscape. The redistribution of the role of the Church and of religion are very much a function of the parallel redistribution of politics. In other words the future of Catholicism in Poland depends on a considerable number of variables, of which only some can be directly influenced by the Church. It remains probable that the Church was more at ease in managing its confrontation with totalitarianism than in developing action to stem its own breakdown. Yet this is precisely the perspective which it has to face in a country that must, in the midst of mounting crises, fundamentally redefine the rules of society. The weakness of the democratic tradition and the gravity of the socio-economic crisis might lead in Poland to popular demands for strong government, and the Church might be tempted to find a place in such new arrangements. This would risk a return to the situation that prevailed between the two wars, a certain form of confusion between religion and the nation-state, the one helping the other with legitimating stereotypes.

It is a problem which Czechoslovakia has not escaped despite its democratic tradition. The movement for Slovak independence has effectively challenged the very existence of the federation. In this situation of tension, Catholicism is possibly being required to act as a vehicle for Slovak nationalism, serving there too as the constitutive criteria for a makeshift identity put together for tactical purposes. It is notable that, in contrast to Bohemia-Moravia, the Christian Democrat movement finished on top in the Slovak parliamentary elections in June 1990. In the same way in Hungary, as noted by Ivan Varga,

> The Christian Democratic Party has rallied social forces and interests that have not clearly discerned the changes that have intervened during the last forty-five years ... the Hungarian Christian Democrats want to resurrect a party and movement which have a direct relationship to (or are subordinate to) the Church.

In a country where according to the most recent opinion polls only ten per cent of the population admits regular religious practice, the Church nonetheless exercises a political influence out of all proportion to its real influence. In addition to the restitution of church property, the Catholic lobby succeeded in obtaining the re-establishment of religious instruction in the schools, and continues to lead campaigns against pornography and abortion.

In taking account of the breadth of the problems confronted by the societies of Central Eastern Europe, the ritual reference to Western democracy – and to the market economy with which it is associated – is far from being enough to assure that a difficult transition goes smoothly. Basically, the collapse of East–West polarity leads to a redefinition of their identities, of the criteria for their constitution and their indispensable points of reference. The privileged vector of this affirmation of identity, the religious, is permanently solicited to lend itself to the enterprise of redefinition, one which goes to the heart of societies in the East as in the West, as well as those in the South and North, and which will continue to do so. Today the whole of Europe is in effect stricken by a triple crisis of transition at the levels of identity, function and control, and bringing with it as many benefits as dangers. The collapse of communism and the resultant wiping out of points of reference are at the origin of a considerable increase in the demand for meaning and direction, particularly in the face of the processes of individualisation and relativisation. This demand for meaning and direction is heard as much in Eastern Europe as it is in the West; and, we can conclude, if the role of a Church is to respond to this demand for direction, then the churches seem to be doing just that both in the East and in the West. But they are doing it by offering solutions requiring normative conformity, even though the individualisation, relativisation and particularisation of the contemporary world produce rejection of such rigid norms.

4
Islam and Christianity in South Eastern Europe
Petya Nitzova

European civilisation stems from the values of Christianity; Islam has always been considered culturally alien and enigmatic to it. Recently Salman Rushdie's case and the 'holy war' rhetoric used by Saddam Hussein powerfully evoked ghosts from the past. The multi-polar world emerging after the end of the cold war period and the ensuing relaxation in East–West relations has still not provided a new enemy image. Because of the historical resentments which have deeply penetrated the cultural self-consciousness of a number of European peoples, Islam fits this purpose very well. The fears – real or imaginary – that Muslim fundamentalism is becoming a major challenge for stability and democracy are widespread.

A closer view reveals that the Muslim presence in Europe is not so insignificant as to be ignored. And now that the new vitality of religion on a global scale causes social and cultural tension, Western-type secularised societies might look at their own socio-historical contexts in a quest for creative options on how to better understand and co-exist with Islam.

A historical overview is indispensable in order to make clear what is meant by Muslim presence in Europe. Islam spread into Europe three times in history, following different patterns and rendering European civilisation interwoven with Muslim–Christian encounters and interaction. The first pattern was the Arab invasion of south-western Europe, which after a couple of centuries of fruitful co-existence ended with a counterattack – the *Reconquista* and the Crusades. In 1492, when Christopher Columbus embarked on his historic journey, he had to depart from a relatively small port, because the shipping lanes of Cadiz and Seville were congested by Muslims and Sephardic Jews, expelled from Spain.

The Mongol invasion of Russia during the thirteenth century led to the formation of a great Muslim state, the Khanate of the Golden Horde. Part of its descendants, mainly Tatars, still constitute pockets of Muslim populations in Russia which spread from the Volga river down to the Caucasus mountains and the Crimean peninsula.

A third encounter between Islam and Europe was the Ottoman invasion of south-eastern Europe, which began when the *Reconquista* was almost over. This third wave of dissemination of Islam in Europe was followed by a lasting process of indigenisation. The Balkans are the part of present-day Europe, where Islam has established itself in a continuous co-existence with Christianity and remains truly adapted to the local cultural traditions.

Today Islam is a basic fact of life in south-eastern Europe. Apart from the Muslim majority of the population of two Balkan countries, Turkey and Albania, there are sizeable Muslim populations in all other countries of the region: former Yugoslavia (Bosnia and Hercegovina, Macedonia), Bulgaria, Greece and Romania.

Orthodox Christianity and Classical Islam
The indigenisation of Islam in the Balkans raises the question what kind of Islam and what kind of Christianity came into interaction to make this confessional pluralism possible. Islam was successful in an area where the Eastern Orthodox faith had reigned for centuries, although Orthodox Christianity and classical Islam have been *traditionally antagonistic.*

From the very rise of Islam in the seventh century the prevailing Byzantine attitude towards it was the feeling of cultural superiority. It remained almost unchanged throughout the historical contacts and interaction between the Byzantine Empire and the Muslim Caliphates: 'Byzantine society was preoccupied with religion .... Not only internal, but even external political events were interpreted in religious terms: Islam was a Christian "heresy"; the Muslims were Arians, Nestorians or simply "atheists"' (Sahas 1971:7).

The intellectual roots of the Eastern Orthodox concept of Islam can be traced back to the works of John of Damascus. Christian by descent, he held a high administrative position at the Umayyad court in Damascus in the eighth century. This provided him with a favourable opportunity to monitor the early rise and might of Islam. Yet his classic doctrinal work, *Source of Knowledge*, and the polemic *Discussion between a Christian and a Saracen* give a distorted image of Islam as a Christian heresy and of Muhammad as a false prophet (*pseudoprophetes:* Sahas 1972, Watt 1991:70–2). The name Saracen itself, used in the Byzantine anti-Islamic literature in the meaning of Muslim, contained deeply derogatory connotations, referring to the Muslims as the illegitimate descendants of Abraham, those who were expelled by Sarrah without grace.[1]

This concept of the inferiority of Islam is taken further and elaborated in the medieval anti-Islamic polemic literature of Byzantine theologians. The main targets of Christian Orthodox misperception of Islam focus on the falseness of Muhammad's prophetic mission, the doctrine of predestination (*kismet*), the materialistic Muslim ethics and the eschatological description of paradise as being indicative of the very low level of Islamic morality.

The Greek Byzantine bias about Islam is very similar to the distorted image of the Muslim faith that took shape in Western Europe between the twelfth and the fourteenth centuries, and to a certain extent has influenced European thinking ever since. William M. Watt summarises it in four points: the Islamic religion is falsehood and a deliberate perversion of faith; it is a religion of violence and the sword; it is a religion of self-indulgence; and Muhammad is the Antichrist. These four aspects of the distorted image of Islam implicate a contrasting self-image of Catholic Christendom as being wholly true and appealing to men rationally; a religion of peace, converting men by persuasion; a religion of asceticism, mortifying all carnal desires (Watt 1972:73–77).[2]

The Arab Muslim conquests, like the later Ottoman invasions, were prepared

---

1. Synonym for Saracens are the terms Hagarenes (the sons of Hagar, Abraham's concubine, rather than a legitimate wife) and Ishmaelites (the descendants of Ishmael, the illegitimate son of Abraham), conveying the same notion of the inferior origin of Islam.

2. Excellent works discussing the Western views of Islam in the Middle Ages are also Daniel (1960) and Southern (1962).

by schism within Christendom. Divided on matters of systematic theology and practice, Western Catholicism and Eastern Orthodoxy had a similar stand towards Islam, characterised by antagonism and rejection. Notwithstanding this commonality on the doctrinal level, they never joined efforts in opposing Islam politically, their own rivalries always gaining the upper hand. The medieval age

> witnessed a contest among Latin Christendom, Orthodox or Greek Christendom and Islam – all three societies born of the Roman imperial collapse, all three claiming explicitly or implicitly to be the new Rome, the new Athens, the new Jerusalem, the authentic heir to Roman political universalism, Hellenistic high culture and the promise of Hebrew prophets. (Haddad 1986:29)

Popular Islam and Popular Christianity

Undoubtedly classical Islam and Orthodox Christianity could not come into successful interaction to find a common home in Europe. But the historical experience of the Balkans is revealing that popular Islam and popular Christianity are by far more compatible than their orthodox versions.

Indeed, official faith in general is concerned with issues like revelation and predestination, heaven and hell, salvation, eternity, believers and infidels. The theological level reached by both Islam and Christianity by the time of the Ottoman conquest in the Balkans was much too abstract and completely beyond the grasp of the ordinary believers. The official faith, be it Muslim or Christian, was professed by the high classes of the medieval society, the officials and the clergy.

The spiritual needs of everyday life in times of vast social and historical calamities were met much more successfully by popular trends within the mainstream religions, concerned with questions of fear, loneliness, guilt, revenge, shame, powerlessness, longing, meaninglessness, disease, crisis and death. On this level of conveying truths popular Islam and popular Christianity seemed neither contradictory nor antagonistic to the extent their orthodox versions did. The religious metamorphosis that took place in these lands refer to the dynamics of popular culture, and not so much to the culture of the elites.

Although Ottoman Islam was Sunni, it was not uniform in its concrete manifestations. As Hichem Djait points out, 'It was Europe that invented the cultural notion of Islam as a totality' (Djait 1985:20). Sufi Islam and the Dervish orders contributed much more considerably to the conversion of the Balkan Christians to the Muslim faith than Sunni Islam itself. The approach of Sufis towards religious life was more emotional than dogmatic and their mystic rituals excited the interest of the lower strata of the local societies. Their devotional life deepened the sense of God's accessibility. The widespread practices of Dervish orders to worship saints and shrines drew Muslims and Christians closer together. Shared performances of offering and oblation to a common saint were frequent.[3]

Reciprocally, some features and phenomena within the Christian faith and church facilitated the dissemination of Islam in the Balkans, too. Although it had dominated the spiritual life of the conquered peoples for centuries, in their everyday practices of worship, Christianity was still mixed with some pagan rituals and beliefs. Besides, a lot of people (especially among the townsfolk), were disappointed by the overt corruption of the Orthodox clergy. The Church's outrageous practice of simony made Islam seem more agreeable with regard to decency and morality.

Although its role has been hotly debated, it can be assumed that the Bogomil heresy also paved the way for the spread of Islam in the Balkans. It sprang to life in an open conflict with the Christian Orthodox Church (Spinka 1933), thus becoming a factor reducing its influence and accelerating its decline in the early centuries of the Ottoman conquest. After being banished from its country of origin, Bulgaria, the heretical teaching spread westwards to Serbia and Bosnia, where it became a state religion (Runciman 1982). The Bogomil heresy penetrated deep into the consciousness of numerous strata of the Balkan societies and alienated them spiritually from the official Orthodox tradition.

The Bogomils rejected many Christian ceremonies, such as baptism, the Eucharist and confession. They outspokenly renounced the cross and the icons,

---

3. Abundant evidence for this is revealed in Hasluck (1929). An intriguing instance of a site of worship shared by Muslims and Christians is the *Demir Baba tekke* in North Eastern Bulgaria. See: Ivanitchka Georgieva (ed) 1991, *Bulgarskite Aliani*, Sofia: Universitetsko Izdatelstvo Sv. Kliment Ohridski, 1991, pp.9–33.

and repelled the eating and drinking of meat and wine. Besides, they were acquainted with the symbolic meaning of the crescent. From their viewpoint the crescent was not the symbol of an alien and hostile faith, but rather the sign of a new victorious heresy, much like their own one. It can be assumed with a great degree of probability that subjected to severe persecutions by the official Church, many Bogomils adopted Islam in a search of tranquility, an escape from the unwanted and imposed rites and symbols of Christianity, as well as economic and social advantages.

The large scale cultural and interfaith exchange that took place in these lands made possible not only confessional pluralism, but also syncretism between the two faiths. The Bektashi order in Albania and the Qizilbash sect in Bulgaria provide striking examples of syncretic practices and phenomena. The Bektashi doctrine has certain points in common with Christianity: the Trinity is represented by the Divinity, Muhammad and Ali, the fourth Caliph; baptism symbolises purity, and sins are confessed; communion is given with bread and cheese; priests are celibate. The Bektashis do not turn towards Mecca in their prayers and do not accept the Quran as a Holy Book. Their rules of fasting differ from the routine Islamic worship and Bektashi women do not have to wear veils (Daniel 1990:8).[4] The Bulgarian Qizilbash do not honour mosques as a place of worship, drink wine and strong drinks during some of their religious rituals and recognise women as full members of their communities.

As a whole, religious compromise in the Balkans was and is widespread. The everyday rites and rituals of Muslim and Christian communities in the countryside are distinct, but not discrete. In certain cases Muslim families secretly baptise their ill children in a hope to restore their health or dye eggs at Easter, paying tribute to an ancient tradition which has never been obliterated. Exchange of sacral food on religious holidays is practised on a large scale. It should also be taken into consideration that polygamy in south-eastern Europe was rare and that women in general have played a much more active role in social life than might be expected.

---

4. The most extensive source on Bektashism is Birge (1937).

Real History and Historical Memory

Regardless of all this, Muslims and Christians alike are more conscious of their differences than of their similarities. Broad public attitudes towards Islam in south-eastern Europe are by and large the product of historical resentments, and history is too imperious a factor to be neglected in the Balkans. However, sometimes it is difficult to distinguish whether it is real history or historical memory that nourishes these resentments.

The residues of the past in today's mass consciousness have their solid objective foundation. Islam was introduced into the Balkans as a result of a foreign conquest and therefore was charged emotionally with powerful political and ideological content. It was regarded by the local population as the religion of the invaders and hence, as an instrument of subjugation. This predetermined an attitude towards the Muslim faith as an alien, hostile and militant one, and this attitude has been internalised in the self-consciousness of the local societies. It is further amplified by the collective memory of compulsory conversions to Islam, practised on a large scale by the Ottoman authorities.

And yet it must be noted that historical memory follows a selective mechanism of highlighting some facts and overlooking others. Academic history provides abundant evidence that many local people adopted Islam voluntarily in pursuit of a more favourable economic and social situation. These proven facts do not descend to the level of historical memory for the critical detachment of real history is not an integral part of it.

Quite often what appears on the surface as contempt towards the alien faith has in reality significant class underpinnings as well. In the case of Bosnia it was the Muslims who enjoyed the privileged positions in the social structure: the wealthy landowning class was Muslim, ruling over serf peasants who were predominantly Christian. The free peasantry that existed alongside the serfs was mainly Muslim, this status having been given to them as a result of conversion. The current backlash against the Muslims has class colouration, since they constitute the greater part of the well-to-do urban population.

The clash between Christian Europe and Ottoman Islam is generally interpreted as a catastrophic event, one that brought about a discontinuity in the process of historical development of the Christian peoples inhabiting this part of the continent. Undoubtedly there was a break, but there was integration too and, it could be argued, a certain continuity. As Bernard Lewis points out,

> When Ottoman rule in Europe came to an end the Christian nations they had ruled for centuries were still there, with their languages, their cultures, their religions, even to some extent their institutions intact, and ready to resume their separate national existence. There are no Muslims today in Spain and Sicily, and no speakers of Arabic. (Lewis 1976:199)

The current conflicts in former Yugoslavia clearly indicate that the old animosities still remain very close to the surface and can easily be inflamed. Nevertheless, in times of relative stability and prosperity the antagonism has been covert and almost absent. During long periods the relations between Muslims and Christians have been characterised by mutual respect and neighbourly assistance. The legacy of tolerance and the legacy of conflict exist side by side in the history of south-eastern Europe.

Since European history has been one of solidification of the nation-state system, European societies have faced the problem how to reconcile their self-images with multiculturalism. For Western Europe the Muslim presence has recently re-appeared on the agenda in the form of Muslim immigrant communities, determined to cultivate their identity. In the years to come they are going to increase in number and significance as a result of the South–North demographic flows. Issues have been raised regarding how these migrants should be integrated into the culture and polity of the nation in which they have come to reside.

Islam is not only a religion, it is an all-embracing way of life. Therefore Muslims in a non-Muslim societal environment show a considerable degree of commonality in their mental and behavioural stereotypes, social attitudes and political values. However much the individual and group behaviour of Muslims is modified by the concrete social status and realities, there is a lasting similarity, generated by their confessional identity.

The Muslim situations in present-day Europe could be approached through the dual perspective of immigrant and indigenous Islam in western and south-eastern Europe respectively. None of these societies has reached the point of amalgamation and full integration of the Muslims within its own fabric. Amidst the non-Muslim social environment, the Muslim communities continue to be distinct and, to a certain extent, marginal. Therefore the growing self-awareness and search for political self-expression of Muslims throughout Europe might set a similar agenda for all European countries, both Eastern and Western.

Reconquista or co-existence? Notwithstanding the resentments, hostilities and misunderstanding between Muslim and non-Muslim communities in South Eastern Europe, their six-century long social interaction provides rich experience of mutual gains in the process of living together. Viewed against this background, 'ethnic cleansing' campaigns seem dangerously anachronistic.

5
Unity in Diversity
Religion and Modernity in Western Europe
Grace Davie

This chapter is in two sections. Using a variety of data sources, the first examines in some detail the broad outlines of religious life in Western Europe. In other words, it concentrates on what Europe has in common, not least its shared religious heritage. The second section adopts a rather different focus. It looks at the way such common patterns as can be established have been differently refracted across a variety of European countries. France and Britain are examined in some detail. The principal theme of the chapter – balancing unity against diversity (across time as well as space) – begins to emerge as the two sections are drawn together.

The European Framework

What, then, do the countries of Western Europe have in common from a religious point of view? There are several ways of looking at this question. First, from a historical perspective. O'Connell (1991), amongst others, identifies three formative factors or themes that come together in the creation and recreation of the unity that we call Europe: these are Judaeo-Christian monotheism, Greek rationalism and Roman organisation. These factors shift and evolve over time, but their combinations can be seen forming and reforming a way of life that we have come to recognise as European. The religious strand within such combinations is self-evident.

It is, however, equally important to grasp the historical complexity of European identity. O'Connell approaches this question by introducing a series of interlocking and overlapping 'blocs' which exist within the European whole. There are seven of these: the Western Islands, Western Europe, Central Europe, the Nordic/Baltic countries, the Mediterranean group, the former Ottoman territories and the Slav peoples. Not all of these will concern us here, but the 'building bloc approach' underlines a crucial aspect of modern as well as historical Europe: that is, to demonstrate 'how complex Europe is and, in consequence, how varied might future unity mosaics prove to be'(1991:9). There is nothing deterministic about the future shape of Europe; several approaches are possible, so too are several outcomes. For the time being, however, we need to stress one point in particular: the shared religious heritage of Western Europe as one of the crucial factors in the continent's development – and, possibly, in its future – and the influence of this heritage on a whole range of cultural values.

Other very different sources reinforce this conclusion. One of these, the European Values Study,[1] provides a principal source of data for this chapter. In contrast with O'Connell's primarily historical approach, the European Values Study exemplifies – for better or worse – sophisticated quantitative social science methodology [2]. Using careful sampling techniques, the EVSSG aims at an accurate mapping of social and moral values across Europe. It has generated very considerable data and will continue to do so. It is essential that we pay close – but at the same time critical – attention to its findings.

---

1. The European Values Study was a major cross-national survey of human values, initially carried out in Europe in 1981, and then extended to other countries worldwide. It was designed by the European Values Systems Study Group (EVSSG). The material used in this chapter covers ten Western European countries. Analyses of the 1981 European material are available in Harding and Phillips, with Fogarty (1986) and in Stoetzel (1983). The British material is written up in Abrams, Gerard and Timms (1985). Other national studies are listed in Harding et al. (1986:xv). A restudy took place in 1990. Published material from this study is beginning to emerge: Timms (1992), Ashford and Timms (1993), though the detailed analyses are still awaited.

2. The European Values Study reveals both the advantages and limitations of survey methodology. These are discussed in the introductory sections of Harding et al. (1986).

Two underlying themes run through the EVSSG study or, more accurately, studies. The first concerns the substance of contemporary European values and asks, in particular, to what extent they are homogeneous; the second takes a more dynamic approach, asking to what extent such values are changing. Both themes involve, inevitably, a religious element. The first, for example, leads very quickly to questions about the origin of shared value systems: 'If values in Western Europe are to any extent shared, if people from different countries share similar social perceptions on their world, how had any such joint cultural experience been created?' (Harding et al. 1986:29). As the European Values Study indicates, the answer lies in deep-rooted cultural experiences which derive from pervasive social influences which have been part of our culture for generations, if not centuries. A shared religious heritage is one such influence.

So much is unproblematic and confirms O'Connell's historical conclusions. On the other hand, as soon as the idea of value change is introduced, the situation becomes more contentious. A series of unavoidable questions immediately presents itself. How far is the primacy given to the role of religion in the creation of values still appropriate? Has this role not been undermined by the process known as secularisation? Can we really maintain in the 1990s that religion remains a central element of our value system? The influence of religion is becoming, surely, increasingly peripheral within contemporary European society. Or is it? These questions, important though they are, go beyond the limits of what is possible here, for they concern the theoretical as well as the empirical questions raised by the evolving place of religion in advanced capitalist societies (Beckford 1989, Hervieu-Léger 1986 and 1993). Rather more modestly, this section will concentrate on the empirical, that is on the principal findings of the EVSSG surveys for a variety of religious indicators.[3]

There are, broadly speaking, five religious indicators within the data: denominational allegiance, reported church attendance, attitudes towards the church, indicators of religious belief and some measurement of subjective religious disposition. These variables have considerably potential: they can be correlated with each other and with a wide range of socio-demographic data. In this respect

---

3. For a fuller picture of this material, essential for any detailed work, *see* the references, note 1.

the survey shows commendable awareness of the complexity of religious phenomena and the need to bear in mind more than one dimension in an individual's (or indeed a nation's) religious life. However, what emerges in practice with respect to these multiple indicators, is a clustering of two types of variable: on the one hand, those concerned with feelings, experience and the more numinous religious beliefs; on the other, those which measure religious orthodoxy, ritual participation and institutional attachment. It is, moreover, the latter (the more orthodox indicators of religious attachment) which display, most obviously, an undeniable degree of secularisation throughout Western Europe. In contrast, the former (the less institutional indicators) indicate a remarkable persistence in some aspects of religious life. The essentials of this contrasting information are presented in Tables 1 and 2 which are taken from the data published by the European Values Study Group (Harding et al. 1981). These tables can be used in two ways: either to indicate the overall picture of the continent or to exemplify some of the national differences to which we shall refer in the second section of this chapter.

First, though, the trends common to the continent as a whole. We should start, perhaps, by echoing one conclusion of the European Values Study itself; that is to treat with considerable caution statements about the secularisation process – particularly unqualified ones – either within Europe or anywhere else. For the data are complex, contradictory even, and clearcut conclusions become correspondingly difficult (Harding et al. 1986:31–34). Bearing this in mind – together with the clustering of the variables that we have already mentioned – it seems to me more accurate to suggest that West Europeans remain, by and large, unchurched populations rather than, simply, secular. For a marked falling-off in religious attendance (especially in the Protestant North) has not resulted, yet, in a parallel abdication of religious belief. In short, many Europeans have ceased to belong to their religious institutions in any meaningful sense, but they have not abandoned,

Table 1 National variations in denominational affiliation and reported church attendance (%)

Country	Predominant Denomination	Denominational Catholic N = 7,071	Affiliation Protestant 3,214	None 1,607	Others and no answers 1940	Church weekly or more often 3073	Monthly 1456	Never 4267	'Score'[1]
Eire	Catholic	95	3	0	2	82	6	4	9.8
Italy	Catholic	93	0	6	1	36	16	21	4.6
Spain	Catholic	90	0	9	1	41	12	25	5.2
Belgium	Catholic	72	2	15	10	30	8	34	3.6
France	Catholic	71	2	26[2]		12	6	57	1.6
Denmark	Protestant	1	92	1	6	3	9	43	0.9
Britain	Protestant	11	74	9	5	14	9	46	2.0
N.Ireland	Protestant	24	66	0	9	52	15	11	6.7
W.Germany	Mixed	41	48	9	1	21	16	20	3.0
Holland	Mixed	32	26	36	6	27	13	41	3.5
W.European Average		57	28	12	2	32	13	30	3.2
All Catholics (N= 7,071)						37	14	22	4.6
All Protestants[3] (N=3,214)						9	12	35	1.5
All non-affiliated (N=1,607)						1	1	87	0.2

Notes:
1. Weighted average across all church attendance categories
2. Two categories coded together
3. Excluding Nonconformists (N=239)

Source: Harding *et al.* (1986: 36–7)

so far, many of their deep seated religious motivations.[4]

Correlations between religious indices and socio-economic variables confirm the existence of socio-religious patterning across national boundaries. For throughout West Europe, it is clear that religious factors correlate to varying degrees with indices of occupation, gender and age (social class as such is more problematic). The correlation with age is particularly striking and raises once again the future shape of European religion. Indeed it prompts the most searching question of the study: are we, in West Europe, experiencing a permanent generational shift with respect to religious behaviour, rather than a manifestation of the normal lifecycle? The EVSSG findings seem to indicate that this might be so:

> The survey data are consistent with the hypothesis that there has been a degree of secularisation in Western Europe. Markedly lower church attendance, institutional attachment, and adherence to traditional beliefs is found in younger compared with older respondents, and data from other sources support the notion that these are not life-cycle differences (1986: 69–70).

If this really is the case, the future shape of European religion may be very different indeed. Hence the significance of regular restudy.

So much for the similarities across West Europe. What about the differences? The first, and most obvious, of these lies between the notably more religious – and Catholic – countries of Southern Europe and the less religious countries of the Protestant North. This variation holds across almost every indicator; indeed they are interrelated. Levels of practice, for example, are markedly higher in Italy, Spain, Belgium and Ireland (closer in its religious life to continental Europe than to Britain) than they are elsewhere. Not surprisingly, one effect of regular mass attendance is a corresponding strength in the traditional orthodoxies through most

---

4. One of the crucial questions raised by the EVSSG material concerns the future of European religion. Are we on the brink of something very different indeed – a markedly more secular twenty-first century? It is, however, very difficult to tell how the relationship between believing and belonging will develop. Nominal belief could well become the norm for the foreseeable future; on the other hand, the two variables may gradually move closer together as nominal belief turns itself into no belief at all (Davie 1990).

Table 2: Traditional Beliefs, with trend comparisons

Believing in	Europe	France	Gt Britain	Holland	W Germany	Eire	N Ireland	Belgium	Spain	Denmark	Italy
God	75	62	76	65	72	95	91	77	87	58	84
A soul	58	46	59	59	61	82	80	52	64	33	63
Sin	57	42	69	49	59	85	91	44	58	29	63
Life after death	43	35	45	42	39	76	72	37	55	26	47
Heaven	40	27	57	39	31	83	81	33	50	17	41
The devil	25	17	30	21	18	57	66	20	33	12	30
Hell	23	15	27	15	14	54	65	18	34	8	31
Re-incarnation	21	22	27	10	19	26	18	13	25	11	21
A personal God	32	26	31	34	28	73	70	39	55	24	26
Some sort of spirit or life force	36	26	39	29	40	16	18	24	23	24	50
Don't really know what to think	16	22	19	17	17	6	8	15	12	22	11
Don't think there is any sort of spirit, God or life force	11	19	9	12	13	2	1	8	6	21	6

Source: adapted from Harding *et al.*(1986: 46-7)

of Catholic Europe.

There are, however, exceptions to this rule and at this point it is necessary to anticipate the discussion in the second part of this chapter. For France displays a very different profile from the other Catholic countries, a contrast that cannot be explained without reference to the particular history of the country in question. The distinctiveness of France's religious history will form one focus of the second section. Other exceptions to a European pattern, or patterns, should be looked at in a similar light; notably the countries which do not conform to the believing without belonging framework. Conspicuous here are the two Irelands. Once again, the particular and problematic nature of Irish history accounts for this; for religion has, regrettably, become entangled with questions of Irish identity on both sides of the border. The high levels of religious practice as well as belief in both the Republic and Northern Ireland are both cause and consequence of this situation. In the Republic especially, the statistics of religious practice remain very high indeed.

Before such particularities are explored in detail one further variation within the overall framework is important. In France, Belgium, the Netherlands and, possibly, Britain (more especially England) there is a higher than average incidence of no religion, or at least no denominational affiliation. Indeed Stoetzel (1983: 89–91), in the French version of the EVSSG analysis, distinguishes four European types in terms of religious affiliation rather than three:[5] the Catholic countries (Spain, Italy and Eire); the predominantly Protestant (Denmark, Great Britain and Northern Ireland); the mixed variety (West Germany); and what he calls a *region laïque* – that is, France, Belgium, the Netherlands and, possibly, England – where those who recognise no religious label form a sizeable section of the population. The inclusion of England in this category is strongly affirmed by the figures emerging from the 1990 data. In many ways this analysis is more satisfying than groupings suggested elsewhere in the European Values material where countries which have very different religious profiles find themselves grouped together.

---

5. Halsey (1985), for example, places British attitudes in a European perspective offering three categories: Scandinavia (Denmark, Sweden, Finland and Norway); Northern Europe (Britain, Northern Ireland, Eire, West Germany, Holland, Belgium and France); and Latin Europe (Italy and Spain). The Northern Europe category includes some very different religious contexts.

In anticipating the following section, we have already indicated one of the severest limitations within the EVSSG data. There is no way of telling from the data why a particular country should be similar to or different from its neighbours. Apparently similar statistical profiles can mask profound differences, a point that we shall explore in some detail with reference to France and Britain. Before doing so a second drawback must also be mentioned. The EVSSG sample sizes for each country are too small to give any meaningful data about religious minorities. It would, however, be grossly misleading to present an image of Europe at the end of the twentieth century without any reference to these increasingly important sections of the European population.

The first of these minorities, the Jews, has been present in Europe for centuries; a presence, moreover, that has been inextricably bound up with the tragedies of recent European history. Nor can it be said, regrettably, that anti-Semitism is a thing of the past. It continues to rear an ugly head from time to time right across Europe, itself a pretty accurate indicator of wider insecurities. Estimations of numbers are always difficult, but there are currently around one million Jews in West Europe, the largest communities being the French (five to six hundred thousand) and the British (300,000). French Judaism has been transformed in the post-war period by the immigration of considerable numbers of Sephardics from North Africa (*see* chapter 6; also Lerman 1989).

Former colonial connections also account for other non-Christian immigrations into Europe. The Islamic communities are, probably, the most significant in this respect, though Britain also houses considerable numbers of Sikhs and Hindus. Islam is, however, the largest other-faith population in Europe, conservative estimates suggesting a figure of six million (Clarke 1988). More specifically, the links between France and North Africa account for the very sizeable French Muslim community (two to three million). Britain's equivalent comes from the Indian sub-continent (1.5 million; *see* also chapter 7). Germany, on the other hand, has absorbed large numbers of migrant workers from the fringes of South Eastern Europe, and from Turkey in particular. The fate of these migrants in the face of growing numbers of East Germans looking for work within the new Germany remains to be seen.

Whatever the outcome of this particular situation, however, one fact remains increasingly clear: the Islamic presence in Europe is here to stay. It follows that Europeans can no longer distance themselves from the debates of the Muslim world. Whether they like it or not, the issues are present on their own doorstep. Admitting that this is the case is not easy for many Europeans, for the Islamic factor undoubtedly challenges the assumptions of European life, both past and present. Peaceful co-existence between Islam and Judaeo-Christian Europe cannot – and never could be – taken for granted. Nor can Muslims accept unequivocally the 'live and let live' religious attitudes assumed by the majority of contemporary Europeans. This, surely, was the problematic at the heart of the Rushdie controversy. Indeed it introduces one of the most urgent questions facing Europe at the present time: the need to create and to sustain a truly tolerant and pluralist society, both in Europe as a whole and in its constituent nations.

Unity and Diversity

The third chapter of David Martin's *General Theory of Secularization* (1978) focuses on the tensions between religion and nationhood within the European situation. It starts from the following premise:

> Europe is a unity by virtue of having possessed one Caesar and one God i.e. by virtue of Rome. It is a diversity by virtue of the existence of nations. The patterns of European religion derive from the tension and the partnership between Caesar and God, and from the relationship between religion and the search for national integrity and identity. (1978:100)

The second section of this chapter will examine these relationships with particular reference to France and to Britain.[6] It will also suggest that recent shifts in perspective – shifts that derive from the implementation of the Single European Act – need to be taken into account in an up to date assessment of the tensions or partnerships between Caesar and God in contemporary Europe.

---

6. France and Britain have been selected as examples of the secularisation process in West Europe in view of the author's familiarity with source material. The process could, equally well, have been documented for other European nations, though up to date material in English is not always available.

But, first, Britain and France.[7] If we look at statistics for believing and belonging in France we find, superficially at least, a pattern rather similar to that in Britain. Around 80% of the French call themselves Roman Catholics, whereas regular weekly attendance at mass is as low as 13%. A further 7% attend mass once or twice a month (Hervieu-Léger 1986). The figures for Britain are not dissimilar (Brierley 1991a, 1991b), though the denominational mix is, clearly, quite different. Only 15% of the British population attend church with any regularity and even fewer in England, but nominal allegiances (especially to the national churches in England and Scotland) remain moderately high.

Such statistics must, however, be carefully interpreted. Why is it, for example, that almost all the indices of secularity are higher in France than in Britain? (Despite their apparent Catholicism, the EVSSG data tell us that only 62% of the French say that they believe in God.) Why, if we look at another set of comparisons, do British Roman Catholics not only practise with greater enthusiasm than French ones, but behave quite differently from a political point of view? Conversely, the French Protestant minority, though tiny, has been disproportionately influential in many aspects of French life. It has, moreover, voted to the Left traditionally, quite unlike its counterpart in Northern Ireland. These differences can only be explained sociologically; that is by taking into account a whole series of interrelated contextual variables (economic, social and political) that derive from a particular national, or regional context. This is the essence of Martin's thesis: that broad social processes – among them the secularisation process – must always be considered in relation to particular historical situations. What, then, are the key contextual variables that have operated so decisively on either side of the Channel?

The greater prominence of secularity in France derives from a religious history quite different from that in Britain. Despite persistent quarrels about various forms of Christianity, Britain has never experienced a major religious split that corresponded with a political divide. In contrast, the French were for generations politically divided about religious questions rather than anything else. The animosity of the early years of the Third Republic culminated in the separation of

---

7. Detailed information on the French situation can be found in Hervieu-Leger (1986) and Michel (1985); for the British case Brierley (1991a and 1991b) and Hastings (1986) are invaluable.

church and state and the establishment of an emphatically secular public school system. The residual bitterness of these quarrels can still be felt; it accounts for the higher profile of anti-religion as well as non-religion in France. It also accounts for the persistence of political allegiances along religious lines right through the first half of the 20th century.

In Britain, a considerably greater degree of pluralism was established at an earlier stage (with substantial Roman Catholic and non-conformist minorities). The existence of such minorities permitted a certain amount of choice between different flavours of Christianity, a choice quite unlike the French obligation to accept Catholicism or nothing at all. This is one major reason, why the 'feel' of British religious life remains qualitatively different from the French, a contrast which persists despite a marked decline in institutional religion on both sides of the Channel. Two relatively recent episodes exemplify these differences. The first, the controversy surrounding the publication of Salman Rushdie's *The Satanic Verses* was, initially, a British affair. Very quickly, however, the episode escalated to the point where it attracted considerable international attention. The French critique reflected very clearly French proccupations about religious matters.

For a start, the divisions in France were far more clear-cut than those in England. Cardinal Decourtray (the president of the French Bishops' Conference) called *The Satanic Verses* 'an offence against religious faith' and lost no time in drawing the comparison with Martin Scorsese's film, *The Last Temptation of Christ*. President Mitterand responded in similar vein: 'All dogmas which through violence, violate the freedom of the human spirit and the right to self expression represent, in my eyes, absolute evil.' The controversy was, it seems, gradually translated into French terms; in other words it became 'part of France's hallowed battle between Christian and Freethinkers' (*The Independent*: 23 February 1989 and 10 February 1990; see also Appignanesi and Maitland 1989). In Britain the response was far more pragmatic, a question of both/and rather than either/or. Much of the debate concerned the law against blasphemy. The Archbishop of Canterbury called for a strengthening of this law to cover religions other than Christianity (*The Independent*: 22 February 1989); others insisted that laws concerning something as outmoded as blasphemy should be abolished altogether. The French, understandably, were mystified by the domestic implications of these exchanges.

A second episode, or rather pair of episodes, confirms these impressions. Not long after the Rushdie controversy became headline news, two or three Muslim girls began to attract attention on either side of the Channel by wearing the traditional Muslim scarf (or *foulard* to use the French term) within school. So much for the similarities. The differences arise in the reactions of each country to the initial gesture. The French were offended, above all, by the wearing of a religious symbol within the public school system, that is within the *école laïque*. The British, in contrast, were unlikely to be bothered about religious symbols *per se* in state schools, for a certain degree of religious life (including religious symbols) forms an integral part of our educational system. Instead we became concerned about school uniform, a peculiarly British preoccupation. Muslim scarves must be rejected because they do not conform to school uniform regulations. Mercifully, the school governors in the British case found a satisfactory compromise: navy blue scarves would, after all, be acceptable. There is, however, a more serious aspect to the British situation, for in Britain there are denominational schools that are, very largely, funded by the state. And if the French were preoccupied about the wearing of a religious symbol in their state schools, in Britain the anomaly was refusing to the Muslim minority what has been allowed, and is still allowed to Anglicans, Roman Catholics and Jews. Such a policy is at best illogical, at worst discriminatory.

If these events exemplify the continuing religious differences between two neighbouring European countries, are there, perhaps, aspects of the present situation which do the reverse? What, to be more precise, will be the effect of greater European unity on this kind of situation? Common rulings from Strasbourg or Brussels on the rights of religious minorities might, for example, iron out some of the anomalies. On the other hand, individual nations could resist such interference, feeling that the regulation of religious minorities is a purely domestic affair. One way or another, we find ourselves returning to two of the recurrent themes in the religious life of contemporary Europe: the problematic of a truly pluralist society and the inevitable tensions between national and supranational levels of control.

The themes need, however, to be set into a broader perspective: the relationship between God and Caesar in a rapidly changing Europe. Looking back, for example, it is clear that the religious factor played a crucial part in the forging of something that we recognise as European. At the same time, this common historical heritage has, undoubtedly, been moulded by a great diversity of contextual pressures into a number of subtypes or national variables, some of which (not least the British case) are very distinct indeed. In the 1990s as European as opposed to national identity emerges, albeit unsteadily, as a dominant theme in European politics, the situation alters once again; a situation within which the religious factor needs to be carefully and continually observed.

On the one hand, we need to ask what 'use' might be made of the religious factor, either by the state or by any number of interested parties. Can, for example, the religious element be pressed into service by the pro-Europeans to emphasise what Europe has in common, or will it be used by their opponents to provide support for discrete and independent nations (or regions) each with its own carefully circumscribed religious sphere, possibly a national church. Either scenario is possible. On the other hand, the argument can be turned around the other way. For the churches (national or otherwise), religious individuals or a wide variety of religious organisations may themselves attempt to initiate – rather than reflect – shifts in public opinion. In other words, the religious factor may operate as an independent variable in bringing about a greater European consciousness, or, conversely, in resisting just such a move. A theoretically informed examination of contemporary events, bearing this framework or frameworks in mind, is, surely, one of the most urgent empirical tasks of the sociology of religion in the 1990s.

6
Jews and Europe
Between Historical Realities and Social Identities
Régine Azria

The European Jewish Past

Jews have long been a part of European history. It is a history punctuated with ups and downs, with periods of tremendous cultural and material enrichment and episodes of destruction and sorrow. To the Jews, Europe has been a privileged soil for the development of the highest forms of spirituality and learning, bringing us back as far as the Middle Ages in France's Southern Provence, in the Rhine Valley, in pre-Inquisition Spain or in Poland. There and then one could find the most radical pietistic groups and movements headed by countless numbers of miracle-maker charismatic leaders, as well as some of the greatest talmudic scholars and most prestigious academies. Europe was also the native place of Jewish rationalist intellectual traditions, be they religious – as with Maimonides in Spain and later on, with Mendelsohn's Jewish Enlightment Movement in Germany – or secular – as with the *Science of Judaism* in Germany too – just to give a few examples, without mentioning the contribution of 'Jewish intelligentsia' to the progress of European culture during the last two centuries.

But one cannot forget either that Europe has also been, and more than once, a favourite playground for Jewish mass-murder and persecution, starting with the medieval crusades and culminating with the Judeocide of the Second World War.

These ambivalent ties which have bound the fate of Jews to Europe for so many centuries have created simultaneously the historical, cultural, political and religious frame and background for the making of a specific entity called Ashkenazi Judaism. The Hebrew word *ashkenaz* means 'Germany' and by extension the migratory space of the Jews from Germany all over Europe, mostly eastward to Central and Eastern European countries. But it obviously means more than a mere geographical territory. It includes in its definition the socio-cultural, intellectual, linguistic, religious, spiritual and liturgical levels of European 'Jewish space'. Of course, one could argue that such a definition makes sense only if compared with or opposed to other specific Jewish spaces, as for example to the Sephardic Jewish world that was enrooted in Spain – *sefarad* meaning 'Spain' in Hebrew – and primarily turned towards, and influenced by, Arabic-Spanish culture.

But, in another way – and herein lies a special point of interest – one is entitled to consider the very notion of Ashkenazi Judaism as objectively worthy of interest. For it appears as one of the first historical expressions of a specific long-lasting European cultural, social, linguistic and religious entity, together and side by side with Christianity. The century-long history of the Jews in pre- and post-emancipatory Europe need not be recalled; it is already well-known. But does one know the deep consequences of the upheavals post-war European Jews had to face?

I have called them 'European Jews' and not 'Ashkenazi Jews' for a purpose. Nowadays, being a European Jew is in no way equivalent to having been an Ashkenazi Jew two or even one generation ago. This can be seen in several ways. First of all, the Holocaust, the *Shoah*, swept this 'Ashkenazi space' away. It does not exist any longer. Post-war generations of European Jews still living in Europe are the orphans of an extinct Judaism. The *Shoah* established a radical gap between what was before – a deep-rooted traditional society, undergoing its own process of secularisation – and what came after – the moral imperative to rescue shreds of a wrecked culture. It created an unprecedented situation within the Jewish world in general and within European Jewry in particular. The continuity of ongoing intergenerational transmission was stopped forever. This is the first reason why Ashkenazi and European Judaism no longer represent one continous, unbroken reality, as they had done before.

The second reason has to do with large-scale migratory flows. Jewish migrations, mostly from Central and Eastern Europe, started prior to the two world wars, partly for economic and political reasons, but mostly due to Anti-Semitism. Some of the Jews just moved westward to France, Great Britain, Belgium or the Scandinavian countries, while a larger number migrated to the Americas, and another part to Palestine, laying the early foundations of the Jewish state. Thus, Ashkenazi Judaism succeeded in throwing out its roots overseas, trying any available destination, even going as far as to antipodal Australia and Southern Africa. After the Second World War the survivors of the nazi camps went in similar directions.

Thus, the very substance of the old European Ashkenazi world could be saved thanks to its flight from Europe. Ashkenazi Judaism ceased to be a primarily European reality to become first an American, then an Israeli one. The demographic collapse of Ashkenazi Judaism was followed hard upon by the advent of another demographic phenomenon that re-shaped and gave new content to European Judaism: the massive arrival of Oriental Jews, mainly in France, in the aftermath of the Israeli–Arab conflict and North-Africa's decolonisation. These are the main reasons why one has to consider nowadays European Jewry and Judaism as new human and cultural realities breaking off with what Ashkenazi Judaism used to be and to mean.

An additional element has now to be taken into account, namely Jewish nationalism under its Zionist form. The appearance and rise of the Zionist idea in Jewish Ashkenazi and European culture, and ultimately the creation of the Jewish state of Israël in 1948, created new objective and subjective conditions for both Jewish consciousness and Jewish existence, as Israel played an important part in the post-war period of reconstruction. It helped to give the Jews the feeling of dignity, pride and safety they so desperately needed after the disasters they had been through. But it also helped to complicate the socio-political game.

We have briefly summarised the main lines of past and recent European Jewish history. To sum up, the first Jewish settlements in Europe take us far back in history, even before the period of the Second Temple, though this never stopped European peoples from considering Jews as foreigners and aliens. This general opinion was shared, mainly due to the fact that, till their emancipation, Jews were not given the opportunity to participate in public life and had to live in separate communities with their own religious laws and customs. Their circumstances forced them to become cosmopolitans. Their fate was tightly dependent on the issues of the general political history of European countries, kingdoms and empires, as well as on the issues of Europe's religious history, be it the victory of the Church over paganism and Islam or the fratricidal struggles opposing the Roman Church to its would-be heretical opponents.

As for the modern and contemporary period, four main elements shaped Jewish European history:

- modern Anti-Semitism, that replaced centuries old Christian anti-Judaism;
- the Judeocide: we have already mentioned that European Judaism was deprived not only of the largest part of its human living forces, but also of its specifically Ashkenazi character, giving place to a new Jewish European reality;
- the rise of European nationalisms, among which its Jewish Zionist expression, Israel;
- the decolonisation of North Africa, the consequence of which was to drive close to three hundred thousand Sefardi Jews to France, who, in turn, gave considerable new life to an exhausted post-war European Jewry and its Judaism.

All these elements together created the necessary but not sufficient ingredients for a widespread identity crisis.

European Jews and the Question of Identity

The identity question did not become relevant till the early 1970s, and was far from being specifically Jewish. It was not a problem for the first post-war generation. But it was for the second. As it happened all over the Western world at that time, the identity crisis rarely, if ever, interfered with vital and immediate issues. It raised questions that only the well-integrated and the well-equipped in economic, social and cultural terms could afford to ask themselves. It happened at that time and not before because the moment was ripe for disillusionment and disenchantment with Western prosperity. This topic is well-known and there is no need to develop it here.

Contrary to previous decades there were no pressing priorities and anxieties for diaspora Jews, no special emergency or threats. North-African Jewish immigration to France and its accompanying problem of integration were being rather successfully solved. The economic prosperity and political stability of the period were an aid in this respect.

Curiously, the catalyst of the whole identity crisis among world Jewry was an event which happened thousands of miles from Europe. Yet it had a deep and psychologically radical effect, that might be compared to that of the Vietnam War on the American people. It was the Six Days War of 1967. Added to the May '68 movement that came after, it had a somehow destabilising effect on Jews.

This identity crisis was probably faced in different ways by Jews according to their country. But there is not much information available on the subject. The present writer knows more about how it was in France. But perhaps France is a-typical. It has its particular past and history. It has the largest West-European Jewish population with close to 600,000 persons. It is unusual also in the demographic predominance of its Sephardic Jewish population over the Ashkenazi. In addition France has its own assimilationist and secular political tradition. But the same could be said about any other European country. For each one, a similar list of national specificities that may have influenced the development of religious or ethnic minorities is available.

This fragmentation of European Jewry into national entities is one of the outcomes of Jewish emancipation. But·it now no longer has the counterweight or former strong social cement that maintained a 'Jewish space' spreading beyond national frontiers and keeping Jews united despite those boundaries. This cement then consisted in the widespread consciousness of a strong Jewish collective identity, in a tightly organised community life and, for the majority, in the acceptance of the Torah. As one knows, these crucial elements are of little weight today for most Jews. The consciousness of this state of things is at the core of the identity quest.

What appears clearly is that the Jewish post-war generation is probably becoming more conscious of its Jewish identity than its parents were. But what appears clearly also is that many Jews do not really know what content they are willing or ready to give to it. After two centuries of social and civic participation, after having experienced the taste of modern values such as democracy, enterprise, individualism and religious freedom, they do not intend to renounce the benefits of the integration which brought them, and go back to ghetto-life and the passive acceptance of the Torah.

Now, the identity quest focuses mainly on the need for clarification and agreement on a number of issues:

- the collective status of Jews within the political and civil societies to which they belong as individuals;
- the nature of their ties to Israel and acceptance by their own state authorities and surrounding non-Jewish cultures of the legitimacy of their solidarity with Israel;
- the content and depth of their own individual ties to Judaism, both in secular and religious terms.

The answer to the first question depends partly on each country's legal arrangements for religion in general – as for instance whether it is a secular, concordat or pillarised society – and for its religious minorities in particular. Examples of both arrangements are *laïcité* in France and the status of recognised religions in Italy. The answer also depends on the extent to which each country admits the principle of the social usefulness of religions and applies it in such fields as health, education and even taxation.

But beside these legal dispositions, one must examine the social reality of Jewish community life. One needs to see if actual participation in Jewish community life and other activities is very low, and whether the concern for Jewish matters is nonetheless real in such circumstances, even when not central. In fact, in the case of France one observes a discrepancy between the Jewish institution's all-embracing community focus and the fragmented reality of the individual Jew's everyday life. For most Jews, the proper Jewish dimension of their life is but one among many others. On the one hand, except for a very few, their social identity is rarely given consideration or organised in accordance with a consciousness of Jewish belonging. In most cases, 'self-identity construction' has replaced 'belonging', in so far as this latter word carries a normative connotation. On the other, this identity construction is done by putting together side by side the various dimensions of social life – the professional, political, ideological, cultural and religious – rather than by merging them into an all-encompassing synthesis. Moreover, the Jewish dimension of this identity is not necessarily the most decisive for their everyday choices. Still, this subjective Jewish identity in the making does demand new ways of Jewish togetherness based on four objective points of reference: the Jewish tradition, Israel, anti-Semitism and the *Shoah*. We will now examine each of them in turn.

The Jewish Tradition

Two preliminary remarks are useful. Firstly, the following analysis has to be considered within a general climate of religious indifference equally affecting Jews and non-Jews. Secondly, the fact needs to be clarified that traditional Judaism focuses on the centrality of the Law rather than on the centrality of dogma. It follows that orthopraxis, or religious practice, comes first and orthodoxy, or religious belief, comes second. The adequacy of one's religious orientation is measured according to the strict keeping of religious rules rather than the acceptance of a creed. A religious Jew is a practising Jew.

Now, the general drop of religious practice among Jews is generally regarded as a long term trend in modern Western societies. But what has made a recent impact is the increase of practice among an ever growing minority. Among this latter, one can distinguish two groups, one of which is the neo-orthodox, made up primarily of young people. In France, their origins are North African. After their arrival in France and usually after having achieved social integration, through education or the professions depending on their age and situation, they were acculturated into an Ashkenazi pre-war pattern of orthodoxy through the missionary Hassidic movement started by Lubavitch. These people have an ambivalent attitude to modernity. However, in spite of its spreading influence within the established community, this neo-orthodox group still remains a small minority which does not exceed a few thousand people.

The second group is more difficult to identify, for it does not appear as a unified group as is the case with the previous one. It is composed of Jews in search of identity. The individuals belonging to this category consider the Jewish tradition as a reservoir of symbols and appropriate behaviours rather than as a normative Law, as it used to be and as it still operates within the first group. Their attitude to tradition is characteristic of modern individualism. They act freely, as autonomous subjects and refuse to take upon themselves the yoke of the Law. The function of tradition is to help one choose one's personal cultural references and social landmarks. One faces here a particular case of normative deregulation. If one agrees with Danièle Hervieu-Léger that religion is 'a particular modality of belief that calls for the legitimising authority of tradition', one has to consider then this attitude to tradition as a departure from religion.

Israel
The second point of reference with regard to Jewish identity is Israel. Much could be said about the ambivalence and the ambiguities of the word, and as a consequence the ambiguous nature of the relation of Jews to Israel. To them, and more generally to the Western world, the word Israel has many levels of meaning: religious, mystical, eschatological and symbolic. But at the same time Israel is a political and national reality, a country with a people and with state institutions.

The central questions raised by the new state can be put this way: does the very existence of the State of Israel constitute an obstacle to the continuation of Jewish life outside Israel's borders? Being bound up with Israel by historical, religious and emotional ties, is it acceptable that diaspora Jews claim to be simultaneously part of a would-be 'Jewish people', distinct from the Israeli people, and also part of the peoples of their many countries of residence?

The answers to these theoretical questions appear of minor importance when one considers the facts. Nowadays, a significant majority of Jews, all over the world and whatever their ideological convictions, do feel a deep and strong concern about Israel. I would even say that, to many Jews, Israel remains the sole and last link beetwen themselves as individuals and Judaism as a whole. Having broken their ancestral bonds to Judaism – community involvement and religious practice – the only thing that remains is Israel. It takes the place of the community and the Torah at the same time.

This widely shared appeal of Israel is, for a large part, irrational. This was shown by the Six Days' War. On this occasion one could have seen and heard, in France and Britain for example, what seemed to be totally assimilated Jews who had kept themselves at a distance from all forms of organised Jewish life for years, suddenly fearing the possible military defeat of Israel. Some of them were even ready to take the first plane, just to be there. Prior to the war the same people would not have given a penny to a fund-raising campaign for Israel. This emotional reaction and sudden consciousness of Jewish involvement was a large-scale phenomenon. As already said, it was at the origin of the identity crisis itself.

At the same time, for most Jews, these feelings and forms of support for Israel do not raise questions about their national belonging and loyalty to their own countries, except for a very few who are more sensitive to what they consider the dangers of ongoing assimilation. This happens in periods of increasing anti-Semitism and xenophobia, which is our third point of reference.

Anti-Semitism

Anti-Semitism is back, if it ever left. In our view, it is the main obstacle to Jews developing full confidence in other people. But it is also one of the main motives for maintaining a full awareness of one's identity. During their long history Jews have been permanently faced with a double threat, a double survival issue, the one more brutal and the other more subtle: anti-Semitism and assimilation. But one observes that anti-Semitism also prevented Jews from complete assimilation. The experience of the Second World War and the persistence of endemic anti-Semitism have contributed to disillusion many Jews as to the possibility of their full acceptance into gentile societies. Considered in this way, one may say that anti-Semitism is a point of reference with regard to Jewish identity, even though a negative one. It compels Jews to self-consciousness and watchfulness.

The *Shoah*

The fourth point of reference with regard to Jewish identity is the *Shoah*. If the previous points appear as rather self-evident, this last one is different in its nature and helps to shed new light on the problems of European Judaism. In the first part of this chapter, I tried to show that the Judeocide had radically upset and changed the very nature of post-war European Judaism. I asserted that pre-war Ashkenazi frames and patterns had disappeared as living and self-producing realities. Now I would like to show this to be the case and also show that the *Shoah* has become a vital identity issue to many Jews.

Owing to its outrageousness and to its immeasurable consequences the *Shoah* has actually taken a place among the crucial episodes of Jewish history, together with and at the same level as the destruction of the Jerusalem Temple and the ensuing dispersion, or the Jews' expulsion from Spain. Such events have a universal significance because of their far-reaching political and ideological effects, for Jews and non-Jews alike. These critical episodes of Jewish history have deeply and lastingly influenced the course of world history. In other words these events can by no means be considered as limited inter-Jewish affairs.

The far-reaching implications of the *Shoah* raise questions about humankind in general, but also about the political and spiritual principles and values at the heart of modern European societies in particular. This is the reason why some thinkers, whether Christian or Jew, felt the need and the necessity to elaborate their philosophical and theological systems with regard to the *Shoah*. On the Jewish side, these intellectual attempts take several shapes. The many theologies of the *Shoah* will not be developed here. Rather it will be shown how the *Shoah* has given birth to a secular myth, at the very roots of a renewed form of Jewish identity.

Most myths of origin begin the history of humanity with a catastrophe, as for instance the biblical deluge. Only after this catastrophe has occurred can the renewal or new beginning be implemented. But the memory of the previous time is not lost; it is preciously kept in the collective memory of the group, like the lost paradise of the Garden of Eden. A similar process takes place within post-war Jews. The *Shoah* represents an eschatological moment of rupture; one that has definitively separated Ashkenazi pre-war Judaism, transmuted into a lost paradise, from post-war Jewish reality.

But a myth can operate only if supported by an authorised memory. Now sometimes an authorised memory can become a challenge to history and objective knowledge. Here we enter the sphere of the sacred. As for Jews this memory of the *Shoah*, and of the lost paradise, is sacred. At least it has something to do with the sacred. Having that in mind helps to understand the reasons why historians dealing with the making of the history of the *Shoah* meet with so many obstacles from the part of some Jewish circles when they try to establish facts. To these Jews the *Shoah* has become sacred, that is untouchable. To them, the making of history, the claim for legitimacy of an accurate and objective approach is not as pressing as the keeping of a sacralised memory.

This sacredness of the memory of the *Shoah* has all the more to be kept untouched as it often represents the last sacred territory. Most Western Jews have renounced their traditions, their rituals, their communities. The only thing Jewish left, that is still alive and meaningful to them, is their bleeding memory of the *Shoah*. No matter how far it keeps them away from reality, this memory is the ultimate reference able to give a value to their lives, for it connects them to their collective past and turns them to the future at the same time. It makes them feel responsible for the generations to come. They may be compared to the temple watchers: to safeguard this sacred thing, this memory, for transmission, they are even ready to struggle and be violent. At least they do their best to be as persuasive as possible. One can see this in the Carmel of Auschwitz Affair. Most poignant is the desperate opposition of Jews to the Christianisation of the Nazi camp; they seem to be afraid that any visible sign, especially Christian, might hide the uniqueness of the Jewish experience of Auschwitz and its invisible memory. In other words they feel this Carmel and its cross as a sacrilege turned against their memory. This instrumentalisation of a sacralised memory works like any other collective memory: it produces a collective identity. In this particular case it works as an ideology for survival. ·

Conclusion

In this chapter, the methodological difficulties one meets when researching minority groups have been omitted from consideration. It appeared more important to concentrate on opening up research into the Jewish presence in Europe and to get it into the general schedule of the sociology of religion and other fields of comparative social research. Finally, I would like to point out that post-war European Jews do not yet constitute a self-conscious and homogeneous entity that could compete with American Jewry. Also, little can be said for the time being about ex-Soviet Union Jews whose collective future is still as uncertain as its past and present condition. *If* European Judaism finds its own way and identity within the 'New Europe', it will no doubt provide a significant field of research and help in the general study of minority groups.

7

Muslim Women in a Western European society: Gujarati Muslim Women in Leicester

Ahmed Y. Andrews

There are perhaps two popular European images of the Muslim woman. One is the dark sloe-eyed houri of the Arabian Nights, while the other is of an oppressed creature weighed down by domestic drudgery and the imposition of Purdah. Although such stereotypes persist, they are, I suggest, somewhat removed from the truth; for the first reflects the fantasy of the orientalist, while the second, although perhaps having some basis in reality, is the political caricature of the militant feminist.

Certainly Muslim women in Europe are oppressed, in the sense that they are generally deprived of political and economic power, but to portray oppression in a stereotypical way is not helpful. Studies of Muslim women in the Netherlands (Speelman 1988), Turkish Alavi and Sunni migrants in Berlin (Wilpert, 1986) and Islam in France (Reeber, 1991) reveal many variations in patterns of religious and other social activity. Speelman (1988:15-16) sees Turkish and Moroccan women in Holland organising both along ethnic lines and across ethnic barriers, in marked contrast to the situation of Asian Muslim women in Britain who usually have little organised contact, be it socially or politically, with Muslim women outside their own ethnic group. Wilpert notes differences between the Alavi and Sunni Turks in Berlin, observing that the Alavis accuse their Sunni countrymen of practising

... extreme segregation and oppression' in respect of the treatment of Muslim women (Wilpert,1986:92). Why do these variations in the observations of the activities of Muslim women exist if, as is often claimed by Muslims, Islam is a unified religion, and if, as many Western feminists state, Islam is the cause of the oppression of such women?

One explanation for these variations is diversity in Islamic theology. Not only are there two major theological traditions, 'Sunni' and 'Shia'; but the Sunnis have four schools of *Fiqh* (Islamic Jurisprudence), *Hanafi, Maliki, Shafi* and *Hanbali*, while the Shias have their own school of jurisprudence which was codified by Imam Jaffar Sadiq (*Jaffari Fiqh*). Furthermore, one can identify within these schools of thought a variety of subdivisions. Given this plurality within Islam, is female oppression related to Islamic ideals, or rather to adherence to a particular school of jurisprudence? This question has not been addressed within the literature on Muslim women in Europe.

Here I wish to suggest that the degree of oppression found among Muslim women is at least partially dependent on the school of Fiqh followed, rather than the ideal teaching of Islam. And that as Islamic jurisprudence has been developed by men, there is at least the possibility that it is the development of patriarchy rather than Islam that is the real barrier to the recognition, by Muslim men, of the rights of Muslim women.

In developing this hypothesis I have sought to create a model of early Islamic society drawing on three sources: The Qur'an, the *Hadith* literature (traditions relating to the recorded actions and sayings of the Prophet Muhammad), and the history of the Islamic community during the time of Muhammad and the first four Caliphs. I seek to compare the activity of early Muslim women with Muslim women in contemporary society, specifically two groups from the same ethnic background (regional/language group), but following different schools of Fiqh. In seeking to study two groups with a common ethnicity, I have endeavoured to exclude the ethnic variable as a cause of any observed differences between the two groups, seeking rather to explain such differences by reference to the school of jurisprudence being followed.

Women's Rights in Early Islam

The sociology of pre-Islamic society is by no means clear. While some have emphasised the nomadic nature of the Arab at this time, Stowasser (1987:290-1), argues that 'Islam is a religion of the city...' and was, '... not a projection of the Bedouin mind', and that the religion arose in a context of social change brought about by economic development. Certainly the status of women in pre-Islamic urban society is unclear, but by the time Islam emerged in the Arabian Peninsular, patriarchy was well established in most of the Middle East. Lerner (1986:212), for example, points out that the exchange of women between tribes was taking place during the Neolithic period both, ' ... as a means of avoiding incessant warfare by the cementing of marriage alliances...' and, '... because societies with more women could produce more children.' The Greek, Roman, and Judaeo/Christian societies which preceded Islam also had well defined patriarchal systems. Mernissi (1975:31) however, argues a case supporting a great degree of independence among women in pre-Islamic Arabia, while Levy (1957:94) concludes that most women were subject to male domination. Finally, Coulson and Hinchcliffe (1978:37) argue that women in pre-Islamic Arabia had no rights, and claim that it was Islam which gave women status.

My own conclusion is that Islam, despite being surrounded by patriarchal systems, was intent on safeguarding women's rights within an evolving patriarchy. It must be remembered, for example, that Khadija, the Prophet's first wife, was a business woman in her own right; evidence that even before the advent of Islam an Arab woman could inherit and control property.

Besides reinforcing the right of women to inherit and to control property independently of their fathers or husbands, Islam also guaranteed to a woman the right to choose her own husband and be supported by him, and also clarified the right of the woman to divorce, while placing strict controls on polygyny by limiting the number of wives a male could have to four (Abdur Rahim 1911:334, 338). Early Islam also encouraged women to develop their education, and have a voice in the political arena (See Fadhl-Allah 1977:49–50, and Al-Ghazaly, n. d.:11).

The collections of *Hadiths* (recorded traditions of Muhammad) and *Sira* (history of the life of Muhammad), reveal not only that women questioned the decisions of the Prophet and the early Caliphs (leaders of the Muslim community), but that it was Aisha, the Prophet's second wife, who controlled the process and work of *Fatwa* (legal ruling) during the period of three of the first four Caliphs. The only *Mufti* (legal adviser) during this period, therefore, was a woman (See Tohmar, 1977:92-174). In addition, it was Aisha who led an army against Ali the Prophet's nephew and son in law. Furthermore Fatima, the daughter of the Prophet and wife of Ali, was also a committed, socially aware Muslim woman.

Coulson and Hinchcliffe (1978:38) state that,

> The hallmark of early Muslim jurisprudence, or at least the Sunni majority, was the principle that the status quo remained valid unless and until it was expressly superseded by the dictates of Islam. Hence the standards and criteria of pre-Islamic customary law were carried over into Islam....

This led to the introduction of strong patriarchal practices as the early Muslims moved out of the Arabian Peninsular. This tendency was strengthened by three other factors.

Firstly, as Nabia Abbott (1985:107) has pointed out, the second Caliph Umar ibn al-Khuttab's opposition to the public participation of women in the Mosque sowed the seed of politico-religious discrimination against women in the 150 years following the death of Muhammad. Second, Aisha's military defeat by Imam Ali resulted in the *Hadith* which states that 'no community will prosper that allows itself to be led by a woman'. Although its validity has been questioned by such scholars as Ali Thanvi (n. d.), it is this *Hadith* that has been used to exclude women from political activity. Thirdly there is evidence that over time many detailed restrictive additions have been made to the *Hadith* literature relating to women. These additions could be the result of post-Islamic man reinforcing a patriarchal system, by suppressing those Islamic teachings which were conducive to the rights of women (Stowasser:286). The end result of all this has been the almost total loss in Islam of the rights which had been given to Muslim women.

The Gujarati Muslim Women of Leicester

In order to discover if *Fiqh* is an important variable affecting the degree of oppression found among Muslim women in Europe, I studied two groups of women from the same ethnic background following different schools of *fiqh* within the Muslim Gujarati community in Leicester. Not only do members of this community fall into the clearly defined groups of Sunni and Shia, but within each group there are both families who have migrated from East Africa, and families who have come directly from India. This study relies, therefore, on empirical evidence obtained from the women of this community, through observation, interviews and a survey using a questionnaire. Each group consisted of sixty subjects divided into three age groups, 16–25, 26–45, and 45+, thereby also reflecting the views of different generations.

Of the eight Sunni Mosques in Leicester, five are dominated by Gujaratis following the doctrine of the Deoband. This Sunni movement was founded by Muhammad Nanautvi and Rashid Gangohi at Deoband, ninety miles from Delhi, now one of the most influential Islamic universities in the world. The Deoband seeks only a limited relationship with the state, and adheres closely to *Hanafi* jurisprudence, attempting to avoid all religious ritual which may be influenced by Shia theology, and the Hindu and Western worlds, concentrating on what may be termed a puritanical style of Islam. It is from this theological division that my sample of Sunni women was drawn. The Shia sample was taken from the Khoja Shia Ithnasheri Community, which accept Imam Ali as their spiritual and temporal leader, and believe that they are guided by a hidden twelfth Imam (see Robinson 1988).

Religious Activity

It is revealing that despite being purpose-built, the mosque of the Sunni group I studied has no separate cloakroom facilities or prayer hall for women.[1] The Shia Mosque did, however, have separate facilities, including a separate entrance to the building.[2]

When questioned about the lack of provision for women at the Sunni Mosque,

---

1. I later discovered that this absence reflected the situation at other Sunni Mosques in Leicester, although there are Sunni Mosques in the United Kingdom that do have facilities for women, e.g. the East London Mosque, London's Regent Park Mosque, and Birmingham's Central Mosque.

2. These facilities were common at other Shia Mosques, e.g. Peterborough, Birmingham, Harrow and Streatham in South West London.

male community members stated that women were not required to attend the Mosque for prayers, and that it was better for them to pray at home. One Mosque elder did admit that he would like to allow women access to the Mosque, but said that the community would not tolerate such an action. The most common comment made to me by Sunni women was that they had no time to go to the Mosque. Perhaps the most revealing remark was a comment made by one *Madrassa* (religious school) teacher who said that, 'If women go to the Mosque they will distract the men from their prayers and be a source of temptation to them.' When it was pointed out that women went to the Mosque in the time of the Prophet, she replied that in those times people were better Muslims.

Women are occasionally allowed access to the Sunni Mosque to hear visiting speakers, usually on a Sunday afternoon when it is not being used by the men. Their most regular activity is a Qur'an study group which meets in one of the women's homes each Sunday afternoon. Young women up to the age of eighteen are allowed to attend the *Madrassa* attached to the Mosque for religious instruction between 5 and 7 pm. daily.

By contrast, Shia women are encouraged to use the Mosque, and in particular many attend Saturday evening meetings, *Majlis*, where they are accommodated in their own hall and can listen to talks given by the *Mulana* or a visiting speaker. In general, women are encouraged to ask questions, via an audio link with the men's prayer room, and to take a full part in the religious activities of the Mosque, including attendance at Friday prayers, where they are segregated from the men. The Shia women are also prominent at the Mosque during the first ten days of *Muharram*, when they remember the events leading up to the battle of Kerbela and the martyrdom of Imam Hussain.

These observations regarding women's attendance at the Mosque were reinforced by their questionnaire responses which showed 57 Shia women attending the Mosque on a weekly basis, as opposed to none of the Sunnis (although four of the Sunni women did state that they attended the Mosque occasionally). Most of the women who attended the Mosque did so in the company of a member of the family, but not necessarily a male member. Reasons given for going to the Mosque produced the following responses: 46 Sunni women went for conferences at the Mosque, seven for prayers[3], and three for special festivals. In contrast, all 60 Shia women claimed to attend the Mosque for prayers, conferences and special festivities.

Neither group of women were represented on the committee of their respective Mosque, and therefore neither group had a direct voice in local community affairs. However, Muslim women in general do not appear, from personal observation, to be as subservient to males in the family as is often supposed, and within the privacy of the home they often make their voice heard on important issues, thereby influencing what the men say in public. While Shia women are encouraged to go on public demonstrations, for example, the one held at Hyde Park in support of the Palestinian *Intifada* on 9th December 1989, and the anti-Rushdie demonstrations; Sunni women are not encouraged to participate in such public events.

In religious observance the women in the Shia group were perhaps closer to the Islamic ideal than the Sunnis, in that they had access to the Mosque. But in both communities there was segregation of the sexes, a practice which seems not to have occurred in early Islam. In the sphere of political activity, both groups were excluded from community politics within the Mosque, although the Shia women were encouraged to take part in wider political activity.

Employment
Roughly half of the women in both groups were employed (33 [55%] of the Sunnis and 27 [45%] of the Shias), but most of the employed Sunni women worked at home (22 [66%]) with only two (6%) in an office and eight (24%) in a factory, while for the Shia group, office work was most common (17 [62%]) with only four (14%) Shia women working at home. The much greater tendency of Sunni women to work at home could be a consequence of the greater freedom allowed in the Shia tradition for women to work outside the home and undergo

---

3. Ten Sunni women in the 16–25 age group attended daily classes at the Madrassa attached to the Mosque.

further education.[4]

Alternatively, since Shia women tend to come from a middle class urban background and most of the Sunni women are from a working class rural environment, it could be argued that class is the major influence on employment patterns. A third explanation was offered to me by a Shia woman from Uganda, who believed that because the society in East Africa had been multicultural, as against that in Gujarat which was Indian, the East African Muslims had a more liberal view of women's employment and education. While country of origin was not a significant factor within either the Sunni or the Shia group, when both groups were taken together there was a marked tendency for those of Indian origin to work at home 19 or (61%), compared with only 7 (24%) from East Africa.[5]

That a large number of Sunni women were employed as outdoor workers in the textile industry was apparent both from the presence of industrial sewing machines in their homes, and by the regular appearance in the streets around the Sunni Mosque of vans delivering and collecting textiles. Employment in this industry is not, however, restricted to Gujarati women, as many Bengali and Pakistanis in Leicester are also employed as outdoor workers. Of those women who were employed in factories, all were employed as machinists in Muslim-owned enterprises, despite the impression I was given that pay and conditions are often not as good as in European-owned factories. When this was pointed out to the women, they all stated that they preferred to work for a Muslim employer as they were able to make time for prayer. They also stated that they preferred to remain within their own communities rather than mix with white women whose language and customs they were not used to.

Purdah

Purdah (the seclusion of women) was never a teaching or characteristic of early Islam during the time of the Prophet, although *Hijab* (the covering of the head of

---

4. Compare the writing for the Deobandi theologian Ali Thanvi (1990) with that of the Shia theologian Mutahher (1982).

5. Of those women of Indian origin, six (19%) worked in an office and a further six (19%) worked in a factory, whereas 13 (44%) of those from East Africa worked in an office, two (6%) in a factory and seven (24%) elsewhere.

women in public) certainly was (see Andrews 1990).

Although neither group practised complete seclusion, very few of the older group of Sunni women ventured outside the Highfields area of Leicester. Among this generation the city centre is still unknown territory, even among women who have lived for over twenty years in the city. Those in the 46+ age group who were economically active were mostly employed in family shops, or as outdoor workers in the textile industry.

The greatest degree of mobility was among the 16–25 and the 26–45 age groups, with women being employed in Asian factories, and using the shopping facilities of the city centre. My informants told me that back home in India there had been little seclusion, with women of all ages helping in the fields. It was also pointed out that such work had been alongside males who were considered to be relatives. Among the Shia group, women of all ages circulated around the city, but most gave up employment upon marriage.

These observations must be seen against two factors. Firstly, the Sunni group is located within a small area of the inner city consisting of some dozen or so adjoining streets, so that they could maintain their social network with very little travelling. The Shia community, on the other hand, is dispersed throughout the Northern and Southern suburbs of the city, with the result that social networks often have to be maintained over longer distances. Secondly, it should be noted that the husbands of most of the women in the Shia community are professional people or factory owners, while the Sunni community is mostly made up of manual workers and shop keepers. This variation in occupational classes will clearly affect the need for married woman to work and contribute to the family income.

Hijab appears uniform among the Shia women, all of whom wear loose fitting coats and black scarfs in public, and at home if strangers are present. The observance of *Hijab* among Sunni women, however, varies considerably, ranging from the wearing of the all-enveloping *burqua* down to the wearing of a scarf or *duppata*, and through to the complete lack of any form of head covering. None of these styles are the prerogative of any particular age group, but are seen to reflect the varying degrees of religious observance found amongst Sunni women.

As a visitor to both Sunni and Shia homes I found that the segregation of men and women varied within the houses of the two groups. Within the homes of Sunni families no segregation appears to take place unless a non-relative is present. When it does occur, the men stay in one room while the women use another. When visiting Shia homes I found that men and women used the same room, but the women kept their hair covered when a male was present who was not a relative.

Control of Income

Within ideal Islam, women had the right to control their own income, and were not expected to contribute to the upkeep of the family. In this study there appeared to be a significant difference in practice between the Sunni and Shia groups. Thirteen (21%) of Sunni women said that they did decide on the disposal of their own income, against twenty five (41%) of Shia women. There was no significant difference in response between the Sunni women who had come from Africa and those who had come from India, nor was there any significant difference within the Shia group. Eighteen (30%) women from the Sunni group and twenty three (38%) from the Shia made voluntary contributions to the family income, while fourteen (23%) Sunni women and four (6%) Shias contributed to the family income out of necessity. A significant difference was therefore observed between the two groups in this respect, possibly reflecting the economic status of the families to which the women belonged.

A number of writers, for example Dhaya (1973), Anwar (1979) and Shaw (1989), have mentioned the fact that the sending of money back to the home country is a feature of Pakistani life in Britain. In particular this has been done by Pakistani men whose families have used such funds to buy property in Pakistan. I was interested therefore to document any such similar activity within my sample. My enquiries showed that twenty five (41%) of Sunni women and four (6%) Shias sent money abroad, and that twenty three (19%) women sent money to India, while six (5%) sent money to East Africa.

In most cases where money was sent abroad by Sunni women, it was done so to assist the family, with the largest amount sent being £80 per month. That most of the women were Sunnis, who were sending to India, appears to me to reflect the fact that the majority of these women were from poor rural backgrounds.

Reasons given for sending money included the following; 'To buy medicine for a sick relative'; 'To help support a young brother at school.'; and 'To help in the maintenance of an Islamic school for Muslim girls.' In relation to the four Shia women, money was sent to help support one relative in India, while money sent to Africa was by way of periodic gifts at such times as the Eid festivals.

The greater number of Sunni women contributing to family income mostly seems to reflect the economic situation of the two groups, in particular the fact that the Shias are mostly urban middle class from East Africa, while the Sunnis are from a rural Indian background, rather than any theological differences.

Marriage

That right of Muslim women to choose their own husband was present in early Islamic tradition, the only criteria being that a Muslim woman had to marry a Muslim, and that there had to be equality of religion between the parties. While the Shias continue to affirm the doctrine of religious equality (Abd al Ati 1977:89) the Sunni schools prefer to follow the pre-Islamic Arab concept of social equality between prospective marriage partners. This latter tradition is used to justify marriage between cousins. Furthermore the *Hanifi* school of Sunni jurisprudence followed by the Sunni community featured in this study is arguably the most oppressive school of Sunni jurisprudence when it comes to forcing women into marriage against their will (see Mughniyyah 1986-7). They maintain that the guardian or parent of an unmarried female is the best person to choose a husband, as the female has no experience of life on which to base a choice.

Likewise women following *Hanafi fiqh* find it almost impossible to obtain *Khula* (Islamic divorce) unless the right of the woman to obtain a divorce has been agreed in principle in her marriage contract,[6] or the husband agrees to a divorce. Sunni women can also apply to a *Sharriah* Court for a dissolution of the marriage should the husband refuse to agree to a dissolution, but in practice, very few Sunni *Ulama* (Religious leaders) will go against the wishes of the man. Where marriages occur within the extended family, e.g. between cousins, there is

---

6. Very few Sunni women I have met even know that they have the right to stipulate clauses in their marriage contract under Hanafi law.

enormous family pressure to preserve the marriage for fear of offending other members of the family or endangering the stability of other marriages within the extended family network.

Within *Ithnasheri* theology, however, a woman can obtain a judicial divorce if she can prove that her husband has failed to maintain her for a year. A sworn statement to this effect is sufficient, providing it is supported by a similar statement from one other person.[7]

There appears to be no significant difference between the two samples with regard to marital status. Forty six (76%) Sunni women were married and living with their partners, as against forty seven (78%) of the Shia sample. Two Sunni women were widowed, compared to three of the Shias, and one Sunni was divorced. The remainder of the two samples were single (eleven [18%] Sunnis and ten [16%] Shias). In both cases, virtually half of the women in the 16-25 age group were married.

There also appeared to be no significant difference in the way that the subjects met their husbands, with 28 (46%) women from the Sunni sample, and 21 (35%) of the Shias, meeting their husbands through parents. One point of interest to emerge was that six Shia women had met their future husband while at university, one of whom had married a Sunni, which is permitted within Shia *fiqh*, and one had married an Englishman who had agreed to become a practising Shia.

When it came to marrying outside the family network, there was a difference between the two groups, with forty six (76%) Sunni women being married to a relative, usually a first or second cousin, as opposed to sixteen (26%) of the Shias. There was a strong tendency to marry a man from the same country of birth as the woman, 42 (70%) of the Sunnis and 40 (67%) of the Shias having done so.

The greater tendency among the Shia to marry non-relatives and, when marrying out of their country of birth of being prepared to marry non-South Asians, could be explained in terms of the Shia theological position of giving religious equality preference over social equality when choosing a marriage partner. But alternatively it might be argued that, being a minority, the Shia are forced to seek marriage partners from outside their ethnic or racial group.

---

7. For a fuller discussion of this see Mutahhery (1982) and Mugniyyah (1988-89).

All the women in both groups received *Meir* (a gift given to a woman by her husband on marriage), and there had been no dowry paid by the women's family to the husband. There was only one reported incidence of a polyganous marriage, involving a Sunni woman from India married to a man twenty years her senior who was a relative and also had a wife in Malawi where he had business interests. Within Shia theology there is also a concept of *Muta* (temporary) marriage, and although the Shia community were aware of its legality within Shiism. I did not come across any evidence of it being practised in Leicester.

Education

Half of both groups had left school between the ages of 16 - 18, and most of these (25 [42%] of the Sunnis and 30 [50%] of the Shias) had been educated in the United Kingdom. Of the women who had been educated abroad, 33 (55%) of the Sunni's and 5 (8%) of the Shias had been educated in India, while 2 (3%) of the Sunnis and 25 (42%) of the Shias had received their education in East Africa. A majority had received their education at co-educational schools.[8] Eight (13%) of the Shias, but only one from the Sunni sample (who had come to the U.K. from East Africa) had attended university.

Sunni and Shia parents had different views about allowing daughters to enter the field of higher education. In general, Sunni parents felt that their daughters would be at risk if allowed to leave home to go on to university, but they were not so worried about letting their daughters go on to vocational training in Leicester. The Shias were less frightened that their daughters would come to moral harm by going away from home to pursue their education. These views may reflect class rather than religious attitudes. Muslims have told me that there is no access to grant-aided University education in India for Muslims, making it difficult for the rural Gujarati Muslims to send their children to university. Consequently, there appears to be little tradition of university education among Gujarati Muslims in India. On the other hand, the predominantly professional East African Shias have a history of higher education within their community.

---

8. 48 of the Sunni group and thirty three from the Shia. When questioned about this apparent lack of single sex schooling, one of my Sunni informants told me that in India, although the schools were co-educational, the boys and girls were segregated within the classroom.

Conclusion

My Leicester study has demonstrated that Gujarati Muslim women do not experience a uniform degree of oppression. Yet all these women are restricted in their public and private lives when judged according to Western concepts of sexual equality, and even when assessed by the standards of equality embodied in ideal Islam. The relative impact of theological or social variables on this pattern has not been established with certainly. Yet the evidence that doctrine affects religious practice, such as access to the Mosque and women's attendance at festivals, seems clear enough, and I would argue that there is enough evidence to support the view that doctrine affects marriage practices. However, continued investigation is needed, using a sample more evenly representative of women from both India and East Africa, before the effects of doctrine on other areas of life can be firmly established.

Perhaps the important point of this study is not the extent to which doctrine affects the social action of Muslim women, but the fact that when doctrine affects their lives, it is doctrine which has been defined by men. It is this fact which some British Muslim women are now starting to address by seeking to define their own role in British Muslim society – not by embracing the Western feminist position, but by asserting their Muslim identity. Ironically this movement is being led by those women who have benefited most from British secularism, young professional Muslim women educated in British schools and in British universities. Such women, although very much a minority, are becoming ever more vocal, forming women's groups such as Al Nisa, and the Women's Manifesto Group of the 'Muslim Parliament'.

This educated elite is starting to question the position of Muslim women in society by referring back to the Qur'an and traditions of ideal Islam, and, as Nielson (1992:52) has noted, '... are beginning to participate in congregational prayers in growing numbers.' Furthermore, they appear to be seeking to apply the virtually neglected Islamic legal concept of *Ijtihad* (independent reasoning)[9] to a re-working of Qur'anic injunctions. How much of an impact such women will have on the lives of their Muslim sisters, such as those represented in this survey,

---

9. Although still used in Shia jurisprudence this is considered by traditional Sunni theologians to have become in-operative in the tenth century.

is yet to be assessed. But that there is a movement from within Islam to improve the situation of Muslim women should go some way to dispel the stereotypical images with which I began. What is needed within the European context to destroy this stereotype is a deconstruction of the term 'Islam', and the development of studies which seek to measure the degree and forms of oppression experienced by the various ethnic and confessional groups found among the Muslims of Europe.

8
Protestant Approaches to European Unification
Jean-Paul Willaime

To understand the positions taken by Protestant churches on the European question and how Protestant churches intervene in relation to European construction, one must first consider the particular situation of Protestant churches in Europe and give an overview of the different international structures set up by the churches on a European scale. We shall therefore examine the following issues in succession: firstly, the historical and structural contexts of the Protestant churches in Europe; secondly, the growing European dimension of inter-church bodies; thirdly, Protestant positions on European unification.

Historical and Structural Contexts of the Protestant Churches in Europe

By meeting the demands of temporal authorities and by entrusting the organisation of the church to the care of the princes, as well as by promoting the circulation of the Bible in vernacular languages, the Reformation led to a pattern where each institutional church was very closely related to a particular territory and a particular culture. In other words, the rise of Protestantism in Europe led to the formation of national or regional churches, with an additional feature being the polarity between Lutheran and Reformed traditions. The (Presbyterian) Church of Scotland, the Netherlands Reformed Church, the Evangelical Lutheran Church of Denmark, the *Evangelische Landeskirche* in Würtemberg in South-West Germany, or the *Eglise Evangélique Réformée du Canton de Vaud* in French-speaking Switzerland, provide good examples.

Ecclesiastical bodies such as these have contributed more or less strongly to the growth of national or regional identities: take for instance the very close relationship that has existed between the Lutheran church and the Swedish national identity, or between Calvinism and the identity of the city of Geneva, or the role of the Kirk in shaping the national identity of Scotland. It is therefore possible to say that Protestantism has played a significant part in the growth of well-defined nation-states in Europe.

Furthermore, the absence of any central ecclesiastical authority in Protestantism has encouraged the development of a kind of 'religious provincialism' among Protestants, still visible today in such bodies as the Protestant Church of the Czech Brethren (in Bohemia) and the Reformed Christian Church in Slovakia; the Protestant Church of the Confession of Augsburg in Silesia; the *Eglise de la Confession d'Augsbourg d'Alsace et de Lorraine* (in France); or, in Germany, the churches established in the *Länder*: the *Evangelische-Lutherische Kirche in Bayern* or the *Evangelisch-Reformierte Kirche in Nordwestdeutschland*, or finally, in Switzerland, the churches established in each canton: the *Eglise Réformée Evangélique de Neuchâtel*, the Church of Zürich, and so on. The way in which Protestantism was allowed to spread and the way in which Protestant churches were allowed to organise are therefore directly related to the configuration of national and regional boundaries. This kind of 'regional ecclesiology' pattern reveals both the denominational diversity of Protestantism (Lutheran churches, Reformed churches, United churches) and the geographical effects of the principle *cuius regio, eius religio*.

In countries where Protestant churches are organised regionally, unity at a national level is often represented merely through a national federative body, as in France or Switzerland, or in Germany where the *Evangelische Kirche in Deutschland*, founded in 1948, is in fact a 'Federation of Lutheran, Reformed and United churches'. However, such is not the case of the *Eglise Protestante Unie* in Belgium, which is more than simply a loose federation.

It is not difficult to understand, then, why European unification is such a challenge for Protestantism given the deep structural, organisational and cultural bonds that exist between Protestant churches and national or regional entities. European unification beckons Protestantism to go beyond provincialism and to adapt itself to a wider geographical area, while Protestantism has already had to spend much energy heaving itself from regional structures up to the level of national structures.

Another important structural aspect is that, owing to its ecclesiastical diversity and its ecclesiology, Protestantism has no central authority, no supranational authoritative body to utter pronouncements on its behalf. Because the World Council of Churches brings together Orthodox, Anglican and Protestant churches, its General Secretary cannot speak in the name of Protestantism; he can only speak on behalf of the WCC, which represents a diverse group of non-Roman forms of Christianity. There is no Protestant equivalent to the Vatican, no structure through which a Protestant religious leader might acquire the status of a head of state and be treated as such.

This situation is not without effect on the degree of recognition granted by European institutions to Protestant representatives: while the Catholic church has its own 'Special Representative from the Holy See' at the Council of Europe and the Vatican enjoys full membership status in the fields of education, culture and sports, Anglican and Protestant churches belong to the three hundred non-governmental organisations accredited by the Council of Europe.

It follows that an Anglican or Protestant religious leader visiting the Council of Europe will not be welcomed on the same level as the Pope. When Archbishop Runcie visited the Council of Europe on 27 November 1989, he was welcomed primarily as the representative of a particular Christian tradition, the Anglican Communion, while John Paul II, on his visit in October 1988, was welcomed only marginally as the representative of a particular church, the Roman Catholic church and more as the great missionary of a universal cause (human rights, peace...), as a kind of 'expert in humankind' (Willaime 1991).

The numerical strength of Protestants in Europe must also be considered. Protestants account for sixteen per cent of the population of the twelve countries that belong to the EEC, and for fourteen per cent of the twenty seven countries that belong to the Council of Europe (which includes such countries as Turkey, Hungary, Czechoslovakia and Poland). The presence of Protestantism cannot be overlooked, but numerically Roman Catholicism is much stronger (63 per cent in the twelve EEC countries, 53 per cent in the twenty seven countries of the Council of Europe).

Historically, we must remember that the 'little Europe' of the Common Market (with its six countries: Benelux, Germany, France and Italy) is not considered favourably by Protestants – especially German Protestants – for to them it meant the Europe of the Vatican, ruled by the Christian Democrats and political leaders who took their orders from the Roman Catholic church (Robert Schuman, Alcide de Gasperi, Konrad Adenauer). At the same time, however, the first president of the European Community was Jean Rey (1902–1984), a Belgian Protestant who was also the President of the European Coal and Steel Community (ECSC) between 1954 and 1958[1]. Should Protestant churches help to strengthen the unity of Western Europe over against the Eastern bloc, or should they rather strive to maintain some links with East European countries? When facing such an alternative, West European Protestants consistently chose the latter course: the maintenance of links with Eastern Europe. It is highly significant that in Germany the unity of the EKD (*Evangelische Kirche in Deutschland*) survived the 1949 partition of Germany between East and West and was maintained through the cold war, even after the building of the Berlin wall in 1961. It was not before 1969, twenty years after the partition, that a specifically East German Protestant body was set up: the *Bund der Evangelischen Kirchen in der DDR* (the Union of Protestant Churches in the German Democratic Republic). It was dissolved in 1991 following the reunification of Germany, and the churches of the Eastern *Länder* were reintegrated into the EKD. Protestant churches have consistently refused to sever the links between West European and East European churches, and for this reason a Council of Churches for Western Europe was never created.

Turning again to the history of the European Economic Community, it is significant that the Northern European countries, with their Protestant or Anglican majorities, only began to enter the EEC in 1973 (the entry of the United Kingdom and Denmark, though it is true that a Roman Catholic country, the Republic of Ireland, entered the Community at the same time). Today, some Protestant

---

1. *See* in particular his views in Rey 1973.

European countries have still not become members of the EEC. Norway, a Lutheran country, is still undecided, and recently a bishop of the Norwegian Church has been warning believers against indulging too much in demonising the EEC, considered by some Protestants to be the latest incarnation of Evil, with the Treaty of Rome ushering in a latter-day Roman Empire, the Beast with seven heads of the book of Revelation (*Réforme*, 15 February 1992). Demonising Brussels and the EEC is also a common exercise of the Revd. Ian Paisley of the Free Presbyterian Church of Ulster. For Ian Paisley, as Steve Bruce remarks, the EEC 'is part of the growth of the Antichrist and in the political sphere what the Roman church is in the religious. Its main purpose is to assist Romanism in its campaign for world domination' (Bruce 1986:229). These kinds of attitudes, though being those of minority groups, testify to the existence in some Protestant minds of a lingering fear that European integration could mean a growing centralisation of power coupled with Catholic supremacy. As we shall see, such fears have had some influence on official Protestant statements on Europe.

Despite Protestant misgivings towards European unification in the West, certain Protestant initiatives deserve to be mentioned. In 1950, at the instigation of the World Council of Churches, a working party was brought together to reflect on the theme 'Christian responsibility in European partnership'. The president of the working group was André Philip (1902–1970), a Protestant and a former government minister who at the time (1949–1951) was the leader of the French delegation to the European Economic Commission. Later, in the early sixties, Protestant lay people involved in the process of European unification in Brussels began to meet regularly. This group was instrumental in the creation in 1978 of a body representing Anglican and Protestant churches in Brussels, and, from 1986 onwards, in Strasbourg. It is called the European Ecumenical Commission for Church and Society (EECCS) and it brings together the churches of the twelve countries of the EEC, plus the Swiss churches.

Alongside Protestant figures like Jean Rey and André Philip one cannot omit Denis de Rougemont (1906–1985), the French-speaking Swiss Protestant philosopher who was extremely active in the field of culture and cultural organisations in Europe and who strongly advocated a federal Europe open to the diversity of its regional communities. Nevertheless, since World War Two, West

European Protestants have always given their preference to the concept of a larger Europe and to maintaining links with the countries beyond the former Iron Curtain. This trend has certainly been reinforced by the relationships between West and East European Orthodox and Protestant churches made possible through the World Council of Churches and the Conference of European Churches. Current revelations about agents of the KGB having infiltrated the Russian Orthodox church and agents of the *Stasi* having infiltrated the Protestant church of the German Democratic Republic shed light on the official positions of these churches and their perception of West European unification as a means used by NATO to further its economic and geopolitical interests.

The Growing European Dimension of Inter-Church Bodies
The main body that has been set up to help Protestant churches in Europe to relate to each other is the Conference of European Churches (KEK). It was founded by Eastern and Western European churches in 1959, when Europe was divided and in a state of 'cold war', in order to build bridges across the borders and with the idea that churches cannot be divided by an iron curtain. The KEK brings together 120 Anglican, Protestant and Orthodox churches in Europe; its member churches work together to promote ecumenism, peace, and respect for human rights, on a European scale. The Roman Catholic counterpart of the Protestant structure is the Council of European Episcopal Conferences or CCEE (the initials of the French name, *Conseil des Conférences Episcopales d'Europe*). The two institutions meet with each other on a regular basis to discuss a variety of issues: the first meeting was held in Chantilly in 1978 and the fifth took place in November 1991 in Santiago de Compostela. The KEK and the CCEE were the twin organisers of the ecumenical gathering for 'Justice, Peace, and Protection of God's Creation' that took place in Basel in May 1989.

It is worth noticing that the KEK is not a Protestant structure as such, since it includes Anglican and Orthodox churches. The weight of Eastern European Orthodox churches was felt in the KEK in the same way as in the WCC: Eastern European churches were opposed to the idea that the KEK should establish contacts with the EEC and the Council of Europe, such institutions being perceived primarily as Western ventures. This has contributed to the rather standoffish attitude of the Protestant churches towards the Twelve and the Council of Europe, and it is only since 1989 that the KEK has finally been able to establish official contacts with the European institutions in Brussels and Strasbourg.

Other structures give a European dimension to ecclesiastical links within Protestantism. I will consider three very different structures, so as to stress the diversity of these links in Europe and how much they are influenced both by denominational characteristics and by Europe's multifarious regional cultures. First there is the Conference of Protestant Churches in Latin Countries (CEPPLE, *Conférence des Eglises Protestantes des Pays Latins*), which was founded in 1956 to bring together the main Protestant churches of Belgium, Spain, France, Italy, Portugal and French-speaking Switzerland, twenty two churches in total, with a majority of Reformed churches. CEPPLE likes to stress what is specific to Latin Protestantism compared with the Protestantism of Northern European countries: Latin Protestantism is often in a minority situation, with live memories of persecutions and discriminations suffered in countries where for centuries the State and Catholicism shared a common cause. The tenth general assembly of the Conference took place in Barcelona in May 1990. Among the motions adopted was the following: 'To organise, in conjunction with other movements, a great Latin gathering to protest against the festivities celebrating the fifth centennial of the discovery of America by Christopher Columbus'.

The second structure is the Conference of the Churches of the Rhine Valley, which brings together the churches of Switzerland, Austria, Germany, the Netherlands and (French) Alsace-Lorraine. It was founded in 1960 and on a certain number of occasions it has issued statements on European questions and on the problem of the pollution of the river Rhine. The third is the Trinational Conference, which was created in 1948 to bring together every two years clergy and lay people representing the British United Reformed Church, the German Protestant Church of the Palatinate, and the French *Eglise Réformée de France*. The last meeting took place in August 1991 in France at the *Centre Protestant de l'Ouest*.

Alongside these territorially-based ventures, there are also structures designed to bring together, on a European scale, churches belonging to the same denomination. European Lutheran churches have organised a number of gatherings

(Tallin, Estonia 1980; Liebfrauenberg, France 1991), and so have European Reformed churches (Vienna, 1987). Additionally there are the European Baptist Federation, which has its congress every five years, and the Central Conference of the Methodist Church for Central and Southern Europe, whose executive committee met in Strasbourg in March 1992 to discuss 'the mission of the church in the context of the new Europe'. These organisations bear witness to the fact that the churches in Europe do relate to each other across the borders, but this tends to happen on a limited geographical or denominational scale, and there is yet no full-blown structure capable of bringing together Protestants on a European scale.

Finally, there is the Concord of Leuenberg, a charter signed by European Reformed and Lutheran churches, which came into effect on October 1st, 1974, establishing full ecclesiastical communion between eighty Protestant churches, the near totality of all Reformed and Lutheran churches in Europe. This is an important manifestation of Protestant unity, on a Reformed-Lutheran scale, for it includes, among other things, mutual recognition of pastoral ordinations, which means that an ordained minister can become the pastor either of a Reformed or a Lutheran congregation. However, the agreement has remained mostly doctrinal and has been followed neither by a common practical testimony by the churches on a European scale, nor by the establishment of a common permanent structure. A general assembly of the churches that have signed the Concord of Leuenberg is to take place in Vienna in 1994. The diversity of European Protestant stuctures makes it difficult for the varied initiatives to be harmonised with each other, and a spirit of competition is occasionally seen to loom between the different endeavours.

A large gathering took place in Budapest in March 1992; the KEK came together in Prague in September 1992; the next assembly of the Concord of Leuenberg will take place in 1994; smaller gatherings – the meeting of the CEPPLE for instance – are also planned in the near future. This short survey of what is currently being organised points to the problem faced by Protestants. Which of these many structures should take precedence over the others? What kind of ecclesiastical links, what kind of ecumenism, what kind of Protestantism ought to be put forward? The logic behind the KEK is not the same as that behind the Concord of Leuenberg or the CEPPLE. This explains why the idea of a European Protestant Synod has not met with unanimous approval.

Protestant Positions on European Unification

In August 1991 in Basel, seventy bishops and other leaders of Protestant churches met together, at the invitation of Bishops Henrik Christiansen (Denmark), Martin Kruse (Germany), Christophe Klein (Romania) and the president of the Federation of Protestant Churches in Switzerland, to reflect on 'the witness of Protestant churches in Europe'. The meeting was organised to try to answer the challenging question that had been raised in some quarters: 'Have Protestants missed the European convoy?' The problem became all the more acute as Protestants realised that Roman Catholicism was acting as a highly visible force on the European scene, in particular through the Pope's travels and speeches. They also realised that they could not agree with John Paul II's views on the evangelisation of Europe.

During the discussions both at the Basel meeting and the Budapest gathering several Protestant leaders considered that to rely on the KEK was not sufficient, and that Protestants needed to meet between themselves so that the European continent might be given the opportunity to receive a clear message from the churches of the Reformation. Following this, a document presenting 'ten theses' was included in the preparatory papers to the Budapest conference, stating the position of Reformed and Lutheran churches on the European question. The purpose of this document is clearly to offer an alternative to the Pope's view of what Europe should become. Here are the headings of each of the ten theses; some of the headings are followed by an extract taken from the text itself:[2]

- Christian witness, not a political vision.
- Our goal is Christian freedom: '...Christian freedom is the foundation of Christian faith of whatever confession and must be the goal of any kind

---

2. The theses as presented here appeared in *Le Messager Evangélique* (Strasbourg) no.8, 23 March 1992, and were drawn from documents provided by the press department of the Budapest conference. I have had personal access to the preparatory documents of the Budapest conference thanks to my colleagues Jean-François Collange and André Birmelé who attended both the Basel and the Budapest conferences.

of evangelisation in Europe.'

- We must accept pluralist society: 'From the Reformation onwards, Christian freedom has led to a growing respect for freedom of conscience and religion and a growing respect for human rights, values now common to the majority of people in Europe and forming the basis for a pluralist political order. We fully accept the pluralist society and wish to proclaim the message of the Gospel in its midst.'

- No 'Christian' State: 'We wish the State to be politically neutral. The Christian gospel is not to be turned into a State ideology imposed on society as a whole. The churches are not to seek a new set of privileges but ought to be committed to a social order where all human beings can live according to their own personal convictions.'

- The churches are a social force among other social forces: 'It is not our intention to abolish the current separation between the church and the social order (and even if it was our intention, we would not have the power to reverse the present situation); we wish to act as a spiritual force among other spiritual forces in a secularised world....'

- We are in favour of practical ecumenism, and against any kind of sectarianism.

- Europe should be seen in the context of the whole world.

- We are called to resist any force that debases life.

- We are in favour of a social charter for Europe: '...to work for equal opportunities for women and men in church and society....'

- Seeking unity in diversity: 'Protestant churches in Europe are in the minority. Moreover, they are divided. The counterpart of pluralism in society is a pluralism of opinions in the Protestant church. The vitality of Protestant churches depends on the vitality of their local congregations. Therefore we encourage every effort designed to help the individual witness of each Christian and the universal priesthood of all believers.'

These ten theses, among other documents and statements from Protestant church leaders, recognise secular society as a fact. The positive effects of secularisation are put forward and Protestantism is said to have played a part in the secularising process. A document published by the Federation of Protestant

Churches in Switzerland and bearing the title 'Europe, Western Europe, Switzerland: Protestant reflections' (1990) affirms: 'The emergence of autonomous reason cannot be explained without reference to Protestantism; the same is true concerning the emergence of democratic institutions.' The same document takes account of the fact that 'Western Christendom is a thing of the past' and that society has emancipated itself from the dominance of religious values.

At the Protestant *Kirchentag* in Dortmund in 1991, Professor Rudolf von Thadden presented eight theses on 'Europe and Christianity' (*Was ist christlich in Europa?*); significantly, one of the theses ran like this: 'Europe has received both from Christian traditions and from the insights of the Enlightenment. Its future lies in the dialogue – possibly in the tension – between the Christian faith and secular society'. Such documents often insist on the plurality of forces that have shaped Europe and on the plurality of religious and philosophical traditions which make up the character of contemporary Europe. Protestant churches see themselves as social forces among other social forces, set in a pluralist society and receiving no special privilege from the State. The idea that the church should be restored to a position of power is clearly rejected.

Hence, Protestant statements are often quite explicit in their rejection of the idea that Christianity should reconquer Europe. At a meeting between the Protestant churches of the Upper Rhine valley on July 4th, 1990, Pastor Michel Hoeffel, the President of the Church of the Augsburg Confession in Alsace-Lorraine (*Eglise de la Confession d'Augsbourg d'Alsace et de Lorraine*), declared in the opening address: 'There can be no question of reverting to a "Christian Europe" where churches would wield some kind of power. The Church must place itself in the service of European society as it gropes towards unity.'

The KEK expressed a similar position in a declaration in May 1990: 'We see a great task facing the churches in Europe: to act as a servant Church, having given up trying to recover a position of power and having abandoned all hope of playing a dominating role in society.' Several articles written in newspapers and journals by Protestant theologians express their disagreement with the Pope's vision of Europe much more openly than the diplomatic statements of Protestant church leaders and official bodies. For instance, Italian Protestant theologian Paolo Ricca insists on the necessity to fight what he calls 'the Roman Catholic tendency to monopolise Christianity' (Brenner 1990).

Commenting on the evangelisation of Europe at a colloquium on 'Protestantism and European construction' which took place in Brussels in September 1991, Swiss Protestant theologian Pierre-Luigi Dubied declared: 'I cannot see how the idea of a re-christianisation of Europe can be accepted as Christian today... Western history is, among other things, the story of the failure of Christendom (Dubied 1991:147). In an article in Le Monde in 1992, the director of the French Protestant weekly *Réforme*, French pastor Michel Leplay, reacted in the following terms to John Paul II's idea of a Christian Europe:

> In a way, I can understand the Pope's optimistic rereading of European history, with the cathedrals, the Renaissance.... But we must not forget another set of historical facts: medieval Christian Europe declared the Jews to be God-killers (the Lateran Council of 1215); Christian Europe invented the Inquisition against the Albigensians; Christian and Humanist united Europe was founded on an in-built spirit of enmity against the Turk and the Jew; and, lastly, the response of Europe to the Reformation in the sixteenth century and the French Revolution in the eighteenth century was often a mixture of violent political repression and passive traditionalism, so that progressive movements finally had to accept a compromise.
>
> In 1992 what conclusions should be drawn from the discovery of America in 1492 and its aftermath? We urgently need to recover our historical memory and use it with discernment. Then we shall be able to build lucid hopes for the future. (*Le Monde*, 22 January 1992)

One last example is appropriate. Eastern European Protestants too are deeply suspicious of the Pope's vision of Europe. At an international gathering organised by the WCC and the KEK in March 1990, Protestants from Czechoslovakia voiced their fears about Roman Catholic expressions of 'triumphalism' in their country, the Roman Catholic church loudly claiming to be 'the hope and the salvation of the Czech and Slovak peoples'. On the same occasion Hungarian Protestant delegates expressed similar fears about Catholicism's ambitious hopes of restoring 'the unity between culture and religion' (BSS 708, 28 March 1992).

However, the positions of Protestant churches cannot be reduced to nothing more than a critical reaction to official Catholic statements. An examination of reports from various official Protestant bodies show that Protestants are interested not so much in a religious approach to Europe as in European co-operation as such, as it is being worked out in Brussels and Strasbourg.

In the above-mentioned Swiss document, as in other documents like the report drafted by Keith Jenkins and Michael Smart (1990) for the British Council of Churches and the Council of Churches for Britain and Ireland, or the report of the Institut d'Ethique (1990) or that of the Fédération Protestante de France (1991), Protestant churches appear to question European authorities on such matters as welfare policies, immigration policies, and the inadequate degree of democracy in European institutions.

Such interventions are rooted in ethical concerns and offer constructive criticism of Europe in the making, by putting forward the demands of the Gospel, such as the call to care for strangers and for the poor. The impression one gets when studying these reports is that Protestant churches fully accept the secular and pluralistic character of their social environment while at the same time exercising a ministry of ethical vigilance. A good example of this is found in the work of the EECCS in Brussels. In November 1990 in Brussels, for the first time, leaders of Protestant and Anglican churches (and church federations) in Europe met with the Commission of the European Communities, and in particular with its president Jacques Delors. The meeting, which was initiated by the churches and organised by the EECCS, dealt with European integration and the role of the churches. Then, in June and November 1991, for a whole day on each occasion, EECCS representatives met with European Commission officials for discussions, with the full support of Jacques Delors, whose wish is that the working-party, which now meets every three months, should also include representatives from other Christian confessions as well as from Judaism and Islam.

Surprisingly, the contacts between the Commission and representatives from Protestant and Anglican churches have been closer and more regular than contacts between the Roman Catholic church and the Commission. Each of the two confessions has its own mode of approach to Europe; the Catholic church shows a preference for the use of diplomatic channels and the media, while the Protestant approach is more unobtrusive with its preference for functional working-parties. The topics that have been discussed up to now between the Commission and the EECCS are the following: political union, relations between the EEC and East

European countries, questions relating to immigration, the Maastricht Summit, the relationship between the economy and ecology (at this point theological aspects were debated between the EECCS representatives and the Commission officials, one of the participants reported).

Before the Maastricht Summit, the EECCS published a declaration containing a number of recommendations on Europe in the making. It stressed the necessity of increasing the powers of the Strasbourg Parliament, and backed the proposal that had been made to create a Council of Regions, even advocating the creation of a 'second parliamentary chamber representing European regions'. Interventions of this kind are directly related to the very process of European unification and to the institutions and rules that are being set up to enable the construction of Europe to proceed smoothly.

The topics that are being dealt with can give rise to a wide variety of opinions, and when the EECCS chooses to defend a particular line of argument there is no certainty that it has consulted the opinion of its member churches beforehand. Pastor Marc Landers pointed to the inadequate degree of democracy in European institutions in a talk that he gave in Brussels in September 1991. He could have mentioned the inadequate level of democracy in the church too and the fact that the discussions with the Commisson might appear to some Protestants as the preserve of a group of ecclesiastical eurocrats or European ecclesiocrats. Moreover, the EECCS document on Maastricht is not a piece of theological reflection. The authors acknowledge the fact that 'the present commentary does not include a theological commentary. However, it is rooted in the involvement of the churches in political questions, the latter being based on theological reflection and theological convictions' (EECCS 1991).

Theology deals with the church and church life. But, when it comes to social ethical questions, Protestant bodies feel justified to exercise in that particular realm a ministry of vigilance and to influence the orientation taken by secular society and by Europe as it develops. The priority given to social ethics is particularly adapted to Protestant pluralism, and, in a way, by sticking to ethics Protestant churches can quietly keep on evading the thorny problem of institutional church unity.

However, involvement in European questions is bound to give Protestant denominationalism a shake and to challenge its pattern of regional ecclesiology. Involvement in Europe is bound to activate the tension in Protestantism between, on the one hand, its theology which rejects any kind of ecclesiastical *magisterium* and which plays down the institutional dimension, and, on the other hand, the practical necessity of making itself heard in contemporary Europe through competent representatives.

Between the KEK, the EECCS, the committee of the Concord of Leuenberg and informal gatherings, it is difficult to tell which should have the privilege of becoming the place where official Protestant statements on Europe are worked out. In this respect the problems met during the discussions towards the possible setting up of a European Protestant synod are highly significant.[3] A number of Protestant churches are not too happy about the idea, either because they feel uneasy about its novelty, not being themselves governed through a synodal structure, or because they fear that it might threaten the progress of ecumenism on a wider scale, or again because, in the words of a German theologian, 'Protestantism does not yet know what it should say to Europe with one voice' (Brenner 1990:13).

While Protestant churches in minority situations from Southern Europe welcome the idea wholeheartedly, Lutheran churches in Scandinavia are opposed to it. The weight of religious and cultural differences between Southern European Reformed churches and Northern European Lutheran churches can be felt clearly. European integration presents Protestantism with the opportunity to build a closer fellowship within itself, but Europe can also become a source of new divisions especially as Protestantism lacks the experience of collective organisation and of speaking with one voice. Protestantism feels involved in ecumenism but while accepting the idea of ecumenical evangelisation, it feels more reluctant towards the idea of a 'Protestant evangelisation'.

Protestant fundamentalism, the most anti-ecumenical branch of Protestantism, shares in some respects the Pope's vision of a restored Christian Europe. Protestant fundamentalist missionaries, for example, are competing with the Jesuits to gain a foothold in post-Communist Russia. But the Reformed-Lutheran tradition

---

3. *See* the opinion of Anglican Vice-President of the KEK, John R Arnold 1992.

of Protestantism does not quite know how to react in such a context. It is caught in a dilemma. On the one hand, to make itself heard, the Reformed-Lutheran tradition would have to set up a representative body, but, according to some, this would mean smuggling Catholic structures into Protestantism. On the other hand, to perpetuate the present dispersal of Protestant energies is to leave the European field wide open for the Roman Catholic offensive. This in-built tension makes it difficult for Protestantism to choose between two alternatives: either to become more institutionalised in order to be able to speak with one voice on the European scene, or to remain faithful to the ideal of Protestant pluralism even if this means a continuance of Catholic dominance on the institutional level.

I have tried to show that the weakness of the Protestant voice in Europe today is not due to recent circumstances but to the way in which Protestant structures developed from the beginning. Protestant provincialism and its lack of international representation are certainly handicaps, but the theological origin of the reluctance of Protestantism to become more organised on a European scale must also be taken into account. All in all, Protestant attitudes towards Europe reveal a great deal about the nature of Protestantism itself.

9
The Principle of Subsidiarity
Liliane Voyé

Just how much power, and of what type, should be reserved for different institutional levels in the fields of politics and religion? These are among the many questions emerging in the process of European union which confront the actors within these respective domains. In other words, the problem is one of the degree of centralisation or decentralisation, of universalism versus particularism. These questions pose the problem of applying the subsidiarity principle and, even more fundamentally, of the interpretation of that principle.

This chapter discusses some of the problems related to that theme, beginning by sketching the history of the principle of subsidiarity, and then with reference to some concrete examples, analysing the problems emerging from the application of the principle in the area of religion – most specifically in the Catholic Church – and in politics.

Origins and Nature of the Principle of Subsidiarity

Although not mentioned by name, the doctrine supporting the principle of subsidiarity was already germinally contained in Thomas Aquinas's writings on the nature of law and the state. But it is generally admitted that the principle itself was explicitly defined in 1931 by Pope Pius XI in his encyclical *Quadragesimo Anno*, where it is expressed as follows:

It is true, as history clearly proves, that because of changed circumstances much that formerly was performed by small associations can now be accomplished only by larger ones. Nevertheless, it is a fixed and unchangeable principle, most basic in social philosophy, immoveable and unalterable, that, just as it is wrong to take away from individuals what they can accomplish by their own ability and effort and entrust it to a community, so it is an injury and at the same time both a serious evil and a disturbance of right order to assign to a larger and higher society what can be performed successfully by smaller and lower communities. The reason is that all social activity, by its very power and nature, should supply help (*subsidium*) to the members of the social body, but may never destroy or absorb them.

The State, then, should leave to these smaller groups the settlement of business and problems of minor importance, which would otherwise greatly distract it. Thus it will carry out with greater freedom, power, and success the tasks belonging to it alone, because it alone is qualified to perform them: directing, watching, stimulating, and restraining, as circumstances suggest or necessity demands. Let those in power, therefore, be convinced that the more faithfully this principle of subsidiary function is followed and a graded hierarchical order exists among the various associations, the greater also will be both social authority and social efficiency, and the happier and more prosperous too will be the condition of the commonwealth. (*Acta Apostolicae Sedis* 1931:2031)

Komonchak remarks that

as a formulated principle, it has a distinctly German genealogy.... *Quadragesimo Anno* was written by Oswald von Nell-Breuning, who has described the powerful influence upon his ideas of Gustav Gundlach S.J. (1892-1963) and other members of the Königswinterer Kreis. On subsidiarity in particular he writes: 'Both the name "principle of subsidiarity" and the formulation in which it is expressed in *Quadragesimo Anno* came from Gundlach. Its material content had long been acknowledged, but it was Gundlach who first formulated this non-rational insight into a principle and gave it the name under which it has since become so famous'. Joseph Pieper was right then in calling subsidiarity an '*übrigens deutsch-rechtlichen Grundsatz*'. (Komanchak 1988:299-300)

The principle was elaborated in response to fear of a growing centralisation of state authority. It was intended to defend intermediary bodies – families, enterprises, associations – constituted on the basis of civil society. As formulated in *Quadragesimo Anno*, the principle is often interpreted in the spirit of nineteenth century liberalism:

> The state is an evil, although perhaps a necessary evil, and its intervention in social and economic affairs must be limited to cases where subordinate bodies are unable or unwilling to perform their own proper function. Thus a proper role devolving to the state alone is not recognised and its activity could theoretically be reduced to nothing. (George 1967:762)

Undoubtedly, the origin of this can more accurately be traced to the Roman Catholic Church's will to affirm its own power and take the initiative when faced with the amplification of the State's powers. With its various levels of internal structuration and given the groups, movements and associations it generates, the Church accordingly defines itself as an expression of civil society not to be imposed upon by the state.

Since it was introduced by Pius XI, subsidiarity has been championed as a first principle of civil society by Popes Pius XII, John XXIII, Paul VI and John Paul II. Pius XII appealed to this principle in relation to crimes against humanity committed by totalitarian regimes (address of the 20 February 1946). In his social encyclicals *Mater et Magistra* and *Pacem in Terris* – John XXIII urged the observation of the subsidiarity principle in economic, social, cultural, political and international life. For his part, Paul VI, in *Populorum Progressio*, saw the implementation of the principle as the condition for the integral development of man and the solidary development of humanity. As to the Constitution of the Council, *Gaudium et Spes*, respect for the dignity and rights of humankind as well as that of the autonomy of various societies is founded upon the principle of subsidiarity. Thus one can say that the principle of subsidiarity is to be found at the very heart of the Church's social documents of the past sixty years.

Despite the frequent and apparently simple use of subsidiarity, commentators have nonetheless run into major difficulties in explaining the meaning of subsidiarity and specifying its implications for civil society. Komonchak has made an attempt. The following elements, he says, are commonly found:

- The priority of the person as the origin and purpose of society: *civitas propter cives, non cives propter civitatem.*

- At the same time, the human person is naturally social, only able to achieve self-realisation in and through social relationships – what is sometimes called the principle of solidarity.

- Social relationships and communities exist to provide help (*subsidium*) to individuals in their free but obligatory assumption of responsibility for their own self-realisation. This subsidiary function of society is not a matter, except in exceptional circumstances, of substituting or supplying for individual self-responsibility, but of providing the sets of conditions necessary for personal self-realisation.

- Larger, higher communities exist to perform the same subsidiary roles toward smaller, lower communities.

- The principle of subsidiarity requires *positively* that all communities not only permit but enable and encourage individuals to exercise their own self-responsibility and that larger communities do the same for smaller ones.

- It requires *negatively* that communities not deprive individuals and smaller communities of their right to exercise their self-responsibility. Intervention, in other words, is only appropriate as 'helping people help themselves'.

- Subsidiarity, therefore, serves as the principle by which to regulate competencies between individuals and communities and between smaller and larger communities.

- It is a formal principle, needing determination in virtue of the nature of a community and of particular circumstances.

- Because it is grounded in the metaphysics of the person, it applies to the life of every society. (1988:301-2)

If the various authors who have examined the question of subsidiarity – be they theologians or canonists, sociologists or political scientists – do not always agree about the exegesis they carry out, they nonetheless all agree in recognising its foundation in the metaphysical affirmation of the eminent dignity of the human person created by God in his image. Humanity is destined to exercise its autonomy in this sense. Responsible for its own development and living up to its potentialities, in perfecting itself, it has as its final end 'striving toward God, plenitude of Truth and Good, which alone are capable of satisfying all the aspirations of [its] intellectual nature' (Piwowarski 1975:105).

But according to the doctrine of the Church, humanity cannot achieve those ends which are proper to it unless members help each other because, according to the Aristotelian and Thomistic thesis, humankind is by nature a social being. The necessary collaboration of its members is the condition for each person's perfection. The groups to which each one belongs – from the family to the state, including all the intermediary lay or religious groups – have as their end the fulfilment of human person and not the inverse: 'They fit into a personalist social order, that is an order oriented towards the human person' (Piwowarski 1975:107). Thus, just as it rejects the extension of the power of the state and its collectivist attempts, the principle of subsidiarity also rejects liberalism, the bearer of an individualism while neglecting solidarity.

Hence, this primacy affirmed of the person in its social nature refers back to two senses of the principle of subsidiarity. The first, positive sense, affirms the rights and duties of people, and similarly of each level of the social order, to define their ends and to be helped by the higher levels in seeking to attain these ends without interference. Secondly, negatively, the principle of subsidiarity denies any higher level group the right to deprive any lower level group and, more fundamentally still, the person, of their responsibility and initiative.

Formulated with a view towards its application to 'civil society', the principle of subsidiarity was not originally intended to be applied to the Church itself, where its application would challenge the hierarchical and monarchical structure of the institution. Yet after the announcement of Vatican Council II, for the first time certain people voiced the hope that subsidiarity might henceforth be considered as a principle of the Church. Moreover they cautioned the Church lest it should be accused of proposing a principle that it failed to apply to itself. According to Komonchak, initial research reveals that the principle was explicitly evoked on three occasions during the second session of this Council. The first concerned the bishops, about whom it was proposed that 'what belongs by divine right to a bishop in the governing of his diocese should be limited as little as possible by the supreme power of the supreme Pontiff; ... bishops themselves, of course, should act in accordance with this principle in their own dioceses' (1988:309).

Subsidiarity was also invoked in debates related to the juridical powers to be given to the bishops' conferences. Finally, an appeal was made, saying that the principle should govern the apostolate of the religious. But in reality the principle of subsidiarity was mentioned explicitly in the texts of Vatican II only in reference to its application to civil society.

Nonetheless, the question was to be raised again and even ended up at the centre of the debates of the first Extraordinary Assembly of the Synod of Bishops, in autumn 1969. The application of the principle to the Church itself was expressly raised in the name of the diversity of local churches and the necessity they quite often experience of having to respond rapidly to local needs. At the conclusion of the Synod, Pope Paul VI admitted that a 'well understood application' of the principle of subsidiarity was a legitimate response to the particular characteristics and exigencies of local churches, but he qualified this recognition with three important reservations: the Church's common good must not be compromised by multiple and excessive forms of particular autonomies; the relative pluralism that may result from the application of subsidiarity must not affect either the faith or the general discipline of the Church; in no case can there be any question of the functioning of the Church being modelled on secular models. But this limited recognition of the principle of subsidiarity on the occasion of the 1969 Synod was not translated into action then, nor in the Code of Canon Law published in 1983. The 1985 Synod of Bishops was the scene of bitter debates about this principle with the English-speaking group pressing strongly for its application and it was closed with a final report, containing this laconic remark in the context of the third suggestion concerning the Church as a communion:

It is recommended that a study be made to examine if the principle of subsidiarity in use in human society can be applied in the Church, and to what degree and in what sense such an application can and should be made. (*Synode Extraordinaire: Célébration de vatican II*, Paris, Cerf, 1986)

A few months later, in June 1986, John Paul II responded to the Synod's request for a study in these terms:

> This is a subtle question, which originated in problems of a social, not ecclesial nature. My predecessors, Pius XI and Pius XII accepted it as a valid principle for social life, whereas for the life of the Church, they pointed out that any application must be made without prejudice to the Church's hierarchical structure; it must also be without prejudice to the nature and exercise of the primacy of the Roman Pontiff. (cited by Komonchak 1988:325)

Things have remained at the same stage, even though the discussion has been intensively pursued in the Church outside Rome, as witnessed by the writer at the *Colloquium* in Salamanca (Spain) in January 1988 with the theme of 'Bishops' Conferences'.

> In summary, one can say that for the church's leadership the application of the principle of subsidiarity to the Church itself has been far from a foregone conclusion. For them the particular nature of the Church allows it to escape rules conceived for civil society. Thus according to Cardinal Ratzinger, the Church is a 'superhuman reality'; and hence, 'Its fundamental structures are willed by God himself and are thus untouchable ... for they are of a sacramental nature'. (Thils 1986:49)

To this objection to the application of the subsidiarity principle to the Church, one which is usually taken by its proponents as decisive, is also added: the evocation of the necessity of unity in the Church and the affirmation of pontifical primacy, which is the guarantor of this unity. Within the Church itself, those who call for the application of the principle of subsidiarity, invoke above all the necessity of taking cultures and specific social situations seriously; they see in its implementation the very condition for the concretisation of divine law; and they consider that the refusal to apply it flows from a simplification and a naïve belief in the existence of a divinely intended pure state of affairs that no human law can regulate (Muller 1988:116–8).

If it has hardly succeeded in blazing a trail through the rigidities of the hierarchical society that is the Roman Catholic Church – subsidiarity has made its way in to the political domain, at least on the theoretical level. Quite specifically, it has been invoked in the context of building European unity and has even been central to the debates to which it gave rise. The principle of subsidiarity not only had its 'intellectual gestation' in Germany where it became integrated into political reflection on the respective powers of the *Länder* and the central state, but this principle was also introduced by Germany into the European milieux where it has become a major reference. The German *Länder*, and more particularly Bavaria, have thus introduced Jacques Delors to the principle of subsidiarity as formulated by the Church for civil society. Perhaps as a result, this principle has today become one of the principal instruments for deciding on the distribution of competencies between the various levels of power within the European Community. But if it is widely used, subsidiarity has many different meanings for the actors who have recourse to it. Schematically, one can say that the European Parliament uses the subsidiarity concept to justify the transfer of power towards the Community, while by contrast, the Conservative government of Great Britain has deployed it to legitimate resistance to any future extensions of the powers of the Community. For their part, the German *Länder* worry about the possibility of being dispossessed of their exclusive competencies and the Union of Confederations of Industry and Employers of Europe (UNICE) justifies, in the name of subsidiarity, its rejection of Community social legislation. The Commission – all of whose propositions are now accompanied by a reference to subsidiarity – has recourse to it on one occasion for justifying its inaction (in social policies, for example), and on another occasion in attempting to enlarge its competencies (in industrial politics, for example) .... Elsewhere, for the regions, bringing subsidiarity to the forefront would allow them to bypass nation-state control and address themselves directly to the Community's central institutions (Pochet 1991:41).

It has become clear that although the principle of subsidiarity has been widely discussed, particularly among European authorities, its application has been anything but simple, to the extent that each actor has used it to defend his or her own point of view and to establish a power base. In analysing the various types of arguments advanced, Adonis and Tyrie (1990) have identified three major types.

Most often deployed is the criterion of efficacy: objectives must be pursued at the level of the Community's institutions where they are likely to be attained. Common interest comes next in justifying the passage of various competencies to central Community control. Finally, the argument of necessity concentrates on the capacity of particular levels to conduct the politics concerned.

Although such arguments are helpful, two observations about them are unavoidable. On the one hand, the distinction between these three criteria is not always that evident, certainly not at the practical level. On the other hand, as these authors themselves underline, nothing is said about which authority should decide and fix who does what when – as is almost always the case – there is disagreement. Hence some suggest another way of resolving the question. Nell-Breuning (1957:225) proposes interpreting the principle of subsidiarity not as a rule for the distribution of competencies but as a rule which governs the burden of proof. Then the principle means that the presumption of competency remains with the individual or with the smaller or less complex group: 'The burden of proof that the individual or the less complex solutions are not adequate and that a more complex solution is more effective or more just remains with those who have the power to set up such solutions' (Kaufmann 1988:288). If this way of interpreting the principle of subsidiarity seems in fact potentially more efficient than that which makes of it a principle of attribution of competencies, in practice, it hardly meets with more success. In the political sphere, as in the religious field, the principle of subsidiarity is more easily formulated than effectively applied. As we will now see, in the Catholic world, it is used by those claiming greater autonomy for the national bishops' conferences, while in the political field, the regions and the European Community use it to legitimate their claims against the nation-state.

The Principle of Subsidiarity and the Religious Domain

In the religious domain, and most particularly within the Catholic Church, the principle of subsidiarity is invoked in order to legitimise the recognition of national bishops' conferences and the attribution of a certain autonomy of administration and decision-making to them. In the name of subsidiarity, these bishops' conferences, it is held, should be made official by situating them formally within the hierarchy of the Church, which, at present, has only two levels: the pope and the bishop. The partisans of officialisation argue that this would probably result in a better adaptation of the positions adopted by the conferences to the specific contexts into which they are inserted. They are more or less explicitly afraid of the controlling capacity of Roman power and insist that the universality of the Church has never meant homogeneity. Those who oppose attributing actual power to the bishops' conferences point to the Church's episcopal structure and fear that these bishops' conferences would in one way or another become autonomous to the detriment of papal authority and the personal responsibility of each bishop.

In the light of these issues, I wish to reflect on two aspects of the question. First, how, in practice, are bishops nominated? Does the pope accept the local proposals, as has long been customary? Or, on the contrary, does the pope impose his own candidates, as has often appeared to have occurred in more recent years under Pope John Paul II? In the first case, the bishops' conferences, whether legalised or not, have in fact considerable autonomy and are able to take into account, if they so wish, the particular circumstances in which they live. In the second case, the bishops' conferences are guided by the pope's choice, and official recognition would not change their orientations very much. It appears that, with respect to papal power, the influence that the pope claims for himself in nominating bishops is more fundamental than the recognition of bishops' Conferences. Everything in fact depends upon who chooses the bishops, and consequently upon learning what influence the pope exerts on the bishop's conferences: that is, the extent of his capacity to impose his views on their pastoral options, and even on their theology.

Secondly, one may ask if 'the rank and file members' of the church consider the pope and the bishops exist on the same level of social reality. I should like to suggest that this is not the case, and that for 'the rank and file', the pope operates more in the symbolic sphere, while the bishops operate more in the sphere of functional relations of the institution. I wish to elaborate this point of view a little further.

No institution, Castoriadis states (1975:161), can be reduced to its functional-rational dimension, that is, to the functions it fulfills in response to the needs of society. Without going into what Castoriadis and others say about the relative and socially constructed character of needs, it is the conclusion of his argument that I shall consider here: no institution, he says, can exist outside the symbolic, which 'assumes the capacity to place a permanent link between two terms so that one "represents" the other'. This representation, which is the symbol, Castoriadis continues, cannot be seen 'as a simple neutral cover, like an instrument perfectly adequate to the expression of a pre-existent content of the "true substance" of social relations, which neither adds nor removes anything'. Nor can it be considered 'as inserted in a rational order that imposes its consequences, whether one wants them or not' (1975:163).

While stressing that the symbolic cannot break away from all reference to the real, Castoriadis insists that it is always relatively autonomous from the real ('in a closed temple, there must be candelabras, but they cannot be reduced to the function of lighting') and that it is devoid of all hierarchisation ('all the details of a ritual are equally important'). And if there is always a functional component, it also always contains something irreducible to the functional, an imaginary component, 'something fabricated' that breaks with the immediate real to give it 'a frame of categories, principles to organise the sensible given', in short, a reference system in relation to which each positions himself and thus avoids anomie (Castoriadis 1975:225ff).

Briefly, Castoriadis' considerations lead me to suggest that bishops' conferences should be seen as operating on a completely different level from that of the pope and thus to challenge the idea that the recognition of an official power for their conferences risks diminishing the pope's power. Indeed, claiming an official power status for the bishops' conferences is based explicitly on the argument that they are apt to have better knowledge of their environment and thus a better adaptation of the rules that they can propose. Thus, they situate themselves on a practical plane and claim to draw their legitimacy from their proximity to daily life.

Certainly, the pope expects his messages to be understood and the rules he enacts to be applied. Consequently he also puts himself on a functional plane. However in reality, the case of the pope is completely different: the legitimacy that is socially granted to him derives much more from the symbolic plane, with its imaginary dimension, than from the level of daily life. His discourse consequently escapes the limits of time and space; the pope can hold to a discourse that is intended to be universal and atemporal because he escapes the rational-functional order. It is certainly as such that this discourse is seized by the masses who throng into St Peter's Square and who assist at the great gatherings that mark the pope's trips: this discourse is a ritual element of a feast (Dobbelaere 1985), that is, of an event that breaks with the everyday routine and that, as such, can contradict it. It is a discourse that is autonomous from reality and that, if it formulates rules, does not see them as being constraints but more as references indicating that the world has a meaning and allows everyone to position him or herself within that order, divergences being only modalities of reference to a rule, to a 'nomos', that is, to a surpassing of chaos.

Although the content of this discourse scarcely corresponds to the facts, it is the level of the discourse that makes for its success as well as that of the very figure of the pope in a world that is said to be secularised. The masses of people who sincerely applaud a speech whose precepts they most often do not apply, act as if there is a tacit agreement on the pope's role: the pope provides principles for the interpretation of reality, but a reality which itself permits a diversity of opinions, and without which one would run the risk of falling prey to anomie. Certainly it is only the church hierarchy and a minority of the faithful who are astonished, even shocked, that the enthusiasm generated by each papal appearance does not result in a change in behaviour that is in flagrant contradiction with the precepts announced by the pope and applauded by a feverish crowd. Implicitly, for the crowd, applauding the pope is to recognise him as the bearer of a rationality other than that controlling the functional in everyday reality. It is a rationality that liberates the crowd from the rationality of everyday reality. The crowd adopts the pope as the enunciator of principles of reference in relationship to which these contradictions take on meaning.

Thus the papacy and the bishops' conferences appear to depend upon two different orders of legitimacy: the legitimacy of the symbolic in its imaginary dimension for the pope; and the legitimacy of the functional and organisational for the bishops' conferences. As such they are not 'in competition' at all, except in an introverted zero-sum vision of the Church in which increasing the powers of the one risks diminishing that of the other. From 'the outside' (and this includes the vast majority of Catholics), the relationship with the pope does not pass through the hierarchical structure of the Church. It radically escapes the bureaucratic order into which, implicitly, discussions of the power of the bishops' conferences would lead it.

Moreover, perhaps the symbolic order is where the Church and religion in general are most expected to appear and where they will find their irreplaceable specificity. For example, is it not in this sense that one must interpret the role that Church leaders are asked to play either on ethical commissions established in various countries trying to respond to the questions raised by genetic manipulation or as 'negotiators' for hostages in Lebanon or in the Yugoslavian conflict? In my opinion, it is not primarily a matter of calling upon technical competence but of appealing to representatives of the principles of an order that is seen to transcend the contradictions generated by science or human antagonisms.

We are suggesting that applying the principle of subsidiarity within the Church (and more particularly, in favour of the bishops' conferences) would probably not diminish the authority of the papacy to the extent that, whether theology likes it or not, he is above all situated at a symbolic level whereas the autonomy which would be recognised for the bishops' conferences would permit them to deal with specific, concrete situations more successfully, without for all that calling the unity symbolised by the pope into question, a unity which, precisely at this symbolic level, would bring about a relatively broad consensus while, in fact, letting certain diversities continue.

The Principle of Subsidiarity and the European Community

The question of centralisation/decentralisation and of universalism/particularism seems to be posed somewhat differently on the political level, notably in regard to the distribution of competences and powers within the European Community – precisely where, as we have seen, this principle has got a lot of ink lately.

The state is at the centre of this debate, caught in the vice between regionalist aspirations and supra-nationalist presumptions. In fact, both of them express identical aspirations and a will to regulate capable of calling into question the monopoly the state has seen granted to it in numerous areas since the end of the eighteenth century.

As Habermas notes, 'State formation secured the overall conditions under which capitalism was able to develop worldwide. It provided both the infrastructure for rational administration and the legal frame for free individual and collective action' (Habermas 1991:3).

The state is thus above all an organisational authority, at the service of economic development and it is only through progressive shifts of meaning that one comes to speak of a nation-state:

> In the classical usage, nations are communities of people of the same descent, who are integrated geographically, in the form of settlements or neighbourhoods, and culturally by their common language, customs and traditions, but who are not yet politically integrated in the form of state organisation. Since the middle of the eighteenth century, the differences in meaning between 'nation'and 'Staatvolk', that is 'nation' and 'politically integrated people' have gradually been disappearing. With the French Revolution, the Nation even becomes the source of state sovereignty, e.g. in the thought of Sieyès.... The meaning of the term nation changed from designating a pre-political entity to something that was supposed to play a constitutive role in defining the political identity of the citizen within the democratic polity.... The nation of citizens does not derive its identity from some common ethnic and cultural properties but rather from the praxis of citizens who actively exercise their civil rights.... So the nation-state and democracy are twins born out of the French Revolution. (Habermas 1991:3–5)

It is precisely this nation-state that for nearly two centuries has found itself at the heart of the political, economic and social organisation of Europe (and, more particularly, the Europe of the twelve) that is presently being challenged both from below and from above – which contributes to explaining the debates surrounding subsidiarity.

Challenged 'from below', the state is in fact seen to be contested – to varying degrees depending on the country and the moment – by the regions composing it, which are often more proximate than 'nations' are to the state, in the original sense Habermas described. If the state avoided this observation until the sixties, it was because it brought about various internal transformations, greeted as representing progress toward the achievement of solidarity, justice and equality: a fairer distribution of material resources (the welfare state) and a democratisation of the political system. In fact, these transformations were chosen in view of their compatibility with the degrees and types of autonomy, identity and freedom that were deemed necessary in a capitalist society and vice versa. (De Santos 1989:11–12)

But today the state seems at once less and less capable of regulating the market on a national level and of coping with the dilemmas of social policy and service provision. The state appears to be producing more and more bureaucracies which enclose the citizen in the helplessness of anonymity and in the non-transparency of ever more sophisticated procedures. Moreover, the political authorities who shape the state are presently going through a grave crisis of representation: appearing less and less credible, hence the growing electoral absenteeism and shifts in voting patterns in recent elections in many countries:

Faced with this loss of effectiveness and credibility the state is suffering from, the 'region' is attempting to re-emerge as the privileged locus of identity and the expression of common interests. Hence it is seeking to climb up to the rank of a political actor closer to the particularisms of the various configurations constituting it, all the while taking 'the universalist principles of democratic states' for granted. (Habermas 1991:11)

While threatened with implosion by the re-emergence of the region, the hegemony of the state is also endangered by the rise of supra-national authorities. More specifically the sovereignity of the nation-states of Europe is being challenged by the progressive setting up of the European Community. At first as the European Economic Community, it set the economic unification of the states which compose it as its primary goal. It has thus played out the same scenario as that which about a century and a half earlier had given birth to the nation-states: in both cases it is a question of providing the economy with the territory required for its full development.

Yet for some time voices have been heard warning lest the social dimension of Europe be forgotten – a warning which seems far from being heeded. On the contrary, little attention is paid to a sense of belonging to the Community, as a place to which so many expectations attach, whose effective importance seems hardly disturbed by the vagueness of its content. Research shows that in all twelve European Community countries (except in Great Britain, where it is practically equal) confidence in Europe is far superior to confidence in the national parliaments: taking the European countries together, 'a great deal' twelve and six per cent respectively; 'quite a lot', forty-five and thirty-seven per cent respectively. Europe therefore appears to be a sort of 'myth for tomorrow'. (*European Values Study* forthcoming). Some even want to rediscover it as a myth of origins, just as some wish to see it in rewriting history and as the Catholic Church, in the person of the pope, has proposed it on various occasions (Luneau and Ladrière 1989:28).

The political domain thus seems to be reorganising itself around regions, bearers both of a certain kind of nationhood and of a project for the concrete mastery, notably economic, of its destiny in reference to a Europe which is mythified, but having uncertain contours.

Conclusion

In the area of religion as well as politics, the principle of subsidiarity appears to be at the heart of the present day reflection about the distribution of authority. The problem of subsidiarity's application is not simply a technical one; it refers also to the question of where solidarities are located and what meanings are attached to different levels of authority.

10
Religion, Memory and Catholic Identity: Young People in France and the 'New Evangelisation of Europe'
Danièle Hervieu-Léger[1]

A central element in the formation of religious identities, whether for individuals or groups, is the process by which the individual or group is notionally incorporated into a line of believers. In modern European societies this process is frustrated by the obstacle of memory. The process of religious identification depends on the group or individual being conscious of sharing with others a stock of references to the past and a remembered experience to hand down to future generations. However, one of the main features of modern societies is precisely that they have ceased to be 'memory societies'. Obviously an antithesis between 'memory societies' ('traditional societies') and 'change societies' (or 'modern societies') must not be drawn too abruptly. But it is not inappropriate to underline the impact of the constant acceleration of history which erases the present by precipitating successive events into the past at an ever-increasing speed.

The corrosive effect of change on the social, cultural and psychological

---

1. Translated by Roger Greaves

evidence of continuity has been part of the process of modernity itself. It is clear that the advent of the age of communication has further challenged the capacity of the individual and the group to identify with a line of believers.

The empirical sociology of religious phenomena has stressed the importance of this characteristic discontinuity in modern societies for the evolution of practices and beliefs. This theme was very present, for instance, in Gabriel le Bras's appraisals of the effects of urbanisation and social and geographic mobility on Catholic observance in France. Many other writers – clearly inspired by Tönnies – discuss the consequences of the disappearance of natural communities such as families and villages on religious socialisation processes and doubt whether any true religious sociability is possible in modern societies. However, theoretical writings on secularisation, most of which take rationalisation as the pivot for their analyses of the relationships between religion and modernity, have rarely put the memory problem at the centre of their analyses. But investigation of modern mutations of memory in relation to the process of shaping the formation of 'lines of believers' and believers' subsequent appeal to those lines of believers – a process specific to religious belief – can offer an equally productive approach to the analysis of religious modernity.

In this chapter, I wish to focus on the particular importance of memory in the formation of religious identities in younger age-groups – those least involved in traditional cultural and religious practices and most involved in the 'instant civilisation' bred by the modern primacy of communication. Sociological studies of youth (Galland 1991) and the family (Roussel 1989) stress the fundamental transformations which have affected the mechanism of socialisation of younger age-groups in societies which give predominant value simultaneously to the primacy of experience, the immediacy of the image and the imperative of individual fulfilment. In general terms these studies found that the process shaping the formation of individual and collective identities tended less and less to follow social transmission channels linking one generation to the one before, and occurred rather as the accumulation and aggregation of successive experiences in which peer exchanges within the same age-group played a decisive role.

This change is of central importance for the formation of religious identities, since it undermines the first principle of the vitality-giving component of religious belief – reference to a line of believers. It is also paramount to the religious institutions, since in the present social and cultural context, it affects their capacity to preserve, reconstitute or constitute the *memory fabric* governing both their capacity to intervene in society and culture, and more fundamentally, their very existence.

How, in concrete terms, are religious institutions responding to this dislocation of the collective memory which is eroding the very basis of their survival? Within Roman Catholicism, the launching of the 'New Evangelisation of Europe' theme provides a good example of the kind of response being implemented. This theme was first mentioned by Pope John Paul II at Compostella in 1984. It was subsequently elaborated upon in his speech to the European Parliament in Strasbourg on 11 October 1988, and finally written into his apostolic exhortation on lay believers *Cristifideles laici* issued in 1989.

The New Evangelisation theme has given rise to keen debate in Catholic circles. It has been diversely interpreted both as an appeal for a spiritual renewal within the Church and as a call for a reconquest of society by the ecclesiastical institution. Over and above the ideological polemics, however, it is clear that the 'New Evangelisation' is a 'variable token', capable of referring to profoundly dissimilar and profoundly contradictory realities, depending on the circumstances of its use and the identity of its users. This is not to say that it is impossible to discover from the Pope's writings and speeches the ideological and geopolitical content of the notion as the Pope himself uses it – sociologists have done just that and their findings are extremely interesting (see Blanquart 1987).

Nevertheless, it is apparent that the impact of the formula as a slogan for action is precisely due to the fact that its ideological implications are perceived very unclearly in Catholic circles. Consequently the term is open to appropriation by individuals and groups who read different meanings into it at different times. The most interesting aspect, from our point of view, is the strategic logic behind the 'ideological availability' of the New Evangelisation theme and the effects that its social availability is likely to cause – from the viewpoint of the (re)constitution of Catholic identity – in the context of the dislocation of memory described earlier. Obviously, it is not my intention to suggest that the Catholic hierarchy and the pope in particular, are deliberately using the 'New Evangelisation' theme as a strategy to revive the failing collective memory of the Catholic community. This aim, if it exists at all, is more likely to exist in a partial and diffuse form, and even then to be located within pastoral objectives which can claim more direct theological and/or political legitimacy. The point which I intend to develop here is the way in which these objectives – whatever they may be – are in fact dependent on an attempt to revive the collective memory using three main methods, which will now be examined in turn.

Reconstructing a utopia of bygone Christian Europe

The utopian dynamic, taken in a precise sociological sense, (see Séguy 1971) has the unique ability to mobilise the collective imagination with a view to constructing a new articulation between the past and a future seen as absolutely new when compared to the rejected present. This dynamic is found in all of the Pope's speeches to Europe, and is expressed via three basic themes: first, modern-day secularised Europe, whose values have been sapped by modern permissiveness, is in danger of losing its soul and hence of destroying itself; second, this danger can only be averted by the fulfilment of European unity along lines which seem impossible today; third this unity itself, the horizon of a true rebirth for Europe, presupposes that the old continent will 'recover its Christian birthright' and rediscover the spiritual roots of its civilisation. In John Paul II's words, 'From memory must come forth prophecy.'[2] The Pope's insistence on the 'Christian roots' of Europe is, as Paul Ladrière has shown, extraordinarily selective: whole sections of the real history of Europe are ignored, particularly those dealing with the formation of modern Europe (Ladrière 1989). This selectivity – used here to renew the formulation of anti-modernism peculiar to intransigent Catholicism – is in itself part of the creative activity of memory, which (in the very way it relates to the past updated to the present) invariably involves a degree of imagination. All memory is a reinvention – and not a reconstitution – of the past. Nonetheless, the more perceptible the absence of the concrete, repetitive and prescriptive presence of the past in the present, the greater the tendency will be for reference to that past to assume a 'legendary' character.

---

2. Speech to the Sixth Symposium of the Council of the European Episcopal Conferences Rome, October 1985.

This being so, it is not surprising that great periods of change, which have invariably resulted in the eviction from the present of the compressed presence of the past, have always been at the same time great periods of utopia. By projecting a past revisited and idealised into a future prophesied as radically different from a radically rejected present, utopia creates, in a mode of renewal, an alternative imagery of continuity – a continuity with a more ancient past than the one imposed by the social conventions of the present, a continuity with a past closer to the pristine source of believers' awareness of the line of belief, a continuity with a happy and beneficent past which contrasts with the woes of the present. Utopia, whether imaginary or practised, renews the imagery of continuity which it enlarges and enriches. In this sense, it makes it possible for people to come to terms with the novelty of the present. This complex set of relationships accounts for the paradoxical capacity that utopias have for eventually resocialising the (imaginary and/or practised) social and cultural dissidence which they orchestrate, with the universe of dominant values whose transformation they in fact accompany.

Insistence on Culture

In the utopian construction of the theme of the 'New Evangelisation', as expounded by John Paul II, reference to the Christian specificity of European culture is a major feature. This insistence on culture is the second method used for remobilising religious memory. In 1980 when the Pope celebrated the fifteenth centenary of the birth of St Benedict in Nursia, he praised the 'pioneer of a new civilisation'. In 1980 again, when he placed Europe under the co-patronage of St Cyril and St Methodius, jointly with St Benedict, he stressed their important role (through the invention of the Cyrillic alphabet) in the constitution of the ancient Slavonic language and the cultures which used it. He returned to this theme in 1985 in the encyclical concerning the two Slav saints, *Salvorum Apostoli*. Insistence on the great wealth and age of European culture stresses the bond between this extraordinary cultural heritage and the spiritual tradition in which it is rooted. In the same spirit, the Pope calls on Europeans to 'bear witness to the profoundly Christian origin of the humane and cultural values which are sacred to them'.[3]

Emotional mobilisation of memory

This twofold move towards a utopian reconstitution and cultural refoundation of the religious identity of Europe is part of a broader initiative for the *emotional mobilisation* of memory. This was found primarily in the huge gatherings held throughout the Pope's visits, at which he deploys all the resources of his personal charisma. The Pope's 'personal visits' to places which are generally *lieux de mémoire* (Nora,1984) – 'places of memory' – for the national or regional localities he is visiting are essential to this emotional intensification of the updating of memory into the present, which is itself used as a means towards the reconstruction of the Christian and Catholic identity. The tone of the speeches made on these occasions is a further factor for emotion, as in the famous rhetorical question delivered during the first visit to France in 1980: 'France, what have you done with your baptism?' – a question which was all the more striking, in emotional terms, for being uttered on the very site in Lyons commemorating early French martyrs. In similar vein was the call made at Compostella in November 1982: 'Old Europe, find yourself again, be yourself, give life back to your roots!' and the emotional content of the speech to the European Parliament in Strasbourg in 1986. In fact, not one of the Pope's European visits fails to provide, in varying degrees of intensity, the twofold (cultural and emotional) reinforcement of utopian compensation which is the Pope's answer to the danger of amnesia threatening the Catholic identity. Affirmation by the group – in the present – of a first person plural experimenting with shared emotions, in principle a method for dispelling the very real dislocation of the collective awareness of belonging to a line of belief which gave rise – in the past – to a common culture.

World Youth Gatherings

Logically enough, young people were a high priority in implementation of this institutional strategy for the recomposition of Catholic memory, or so we may assume, in endeavouring to provide a sociological account of the importance the

---

3. Speech delivered during the visit to Austria, 10–13 September 1983.

Catholic hierarchy place on the World Youth Gatherings held each alternate summer. An initial invitation to the young people of Europe to travel to Rome for Whitsun was made by John Paul II in 1984. Around 300,000 young people turned up. This success led to the decision that a World Youth Day would be held every year on the same Sunday. In addition a major gathering would bring young people together in the Pope's presence every other year. The first was held in Rome in 1985. The second attracted 600,000 young people to Compostella, Spain in the summer of 1989 and an estimated 1.5 million young people flocked to the shrine of the Black Madonna in Czestochowa, Poland in August 1991.

The Institution's Interpretation

What does the institution, and what do the young people themselves, see as the real purpose of these gatherings? Is there a correlation between the aim of the institution to use the gatherings as a method of instruction in Catholic identity and the pilgrims' own accounts of the venture? In an attempt to throw light on these questions, I collected literature produced on this occasion (pamphlets, pilgrimage documents, guide books, and other material) and a number of professional and amateur videos. I also interviewed a series of enrolled young pilgrims, and processed around a hundred questionnaires filled out by pilgrims in their home dioceses after their return.[4]

The enrolment system is in itself a sign that the French church hierarchy intended to control the organisation of participation in the pilgrimage. In fact, this was directed not so much against the unpredictable spontaneity of the young pilgrims themselves against the autonomous initiatives of the extremely active religious entrepreneurs – the charismatic movements in particular – who had completely dominated the proceedings in Compostella. At all events, the gathering was presented from the outset as an institutionally regulated venture run by the *Secrétariat del l'Episcopat* in conjunction with all of the French dioceses, which

---

4. This data related only to the 23,450 French young people officially enrolled in the pilgrimage by the various nationwide organisations which took part. There were 500 busloads of around 50 young people and from 100 to 300 other vehicles. The official figure does not include the 1000-2000 French boys and girls enrolled in international groups run by the Salesians, Néo-Catéchuménat etc. and those not enrolled at all but who attended – a total of around 75,000 young people.

ultimately accounted for 13,240 pilgrims, and all of the movements and organisations recognised by the Catholic Church.[5] This decentralised, but firmly controlled, institutional framework favoured massive enrolments from young Catholics already involved in church activities, youth groups and other structures. Each of the participating groups was ultimately able to choose its own approach to the general theme of the pilgrimage chosen from St Paul's Epistle to the Romans (8:15): 'Ye have received the spirit of adoption'.

As an example of these participating groups, I shall take the *Communauté de l'Emmanuel*, which took 2,000 young people to Czestochowa. The booklet issued to its pilgrims provides extremely interesting information about the practical implementation of the triple strategy of utopian reconstruction, cultural reinforcement and emotionalisation of Catholic identity among young people. The overall objective suggested to the participants is to discover that 'being adopted by God means [...] welcoming the Holy Spirit, being guided by the Spirit, being responsive to the Spirit's action in our personal history and the history of the world'. This perception of the Spirit's intervention in history is explicitly linked by the Emmanuel leaders with the current political turmoil in Europe:

> Let us thank God [...]. We are in a time of upheaval and foundation. We are building a new world. Recent events have shown this to be so. The fall of the Berlin wall is the symbol of a new Europe. Suddenly, entire nations which had ceased to communicate are getting together again, talking to each other, holding out their hands to each other. Tomorrow's Europe will be very different from yesterday's, and it will be our task to build it. Hence, by God's providence, our generation has an immense responsibility on its hands. If we fail to act, or if we act wrongly, the Europe which we shall build will be materialistic, selfish, self-centred, and our old demons – pride, scorn for others, violence, ideological error – will return. Once more, we are in danger of war and separation. [...] But that is not the Europe which we wish to build. On the contrary, we wish to share in the building of a juster and more fraternal world.[6]

---

5. Catholic Action groups, Scout groups, prayer groups, charismatic groups, and other groups which together accounted for 9,115 pilgrims.

6. From the introduction to the booklet *Forum itinérant des jeunes* distributed by the *Communauté de l'Emmanuel*.

The theme of a Europe endangered on all sides by change is matched antithetically by the theme of a radically new world which young Christians have responsibility for preparing. As to the resources they can call on, the booklet proposes an initial set of possibilities.

It opens with a long description of the journey ahead. The intention is to use the several days spent crossing Europe to immerse the young pilgrims in the early Christian history and geography of the old continent. Consequently, everyone receives a comprehensive guidebook designed for a special kind of tourism. A series of well-informed chapters provides all the information needed to 'make intelligent' use of the journey – major episodes from history, population data, details of the cultural, architectural and other treasures of each region on the itinerary. However, each of the stopovers on this cultural journey across Europe has religious significance – Paray-le-Monial, Altötting, Beauraing, Velehrad, Czestochowa, Prague – and several have strong connections with the Virgin, hence with the Catholic church, as places of apparitions and miracles. And history is of course presented selectively to insist on the intrinsically Catholic construction of Europe. To give just one example, the section on Prague commemorates St Norbert, the founder of the White Canons, but does not even mention John Huss.[7]

The second part of the booklet, entitled *Enseignments* ('teachings'), is a short Catholic catechesis under four headings: Consecration to Mary, Adoration, Compassion and Evangelisation. This is followed by a series of texts, including one by Vaclav Havel which insistently refers to the necessary moral regeneration of the country after forty years of communist totalitarianism and stresses the need for politics to be subordinate to morals. Another text, by Chiara Lubich, the founder of the Focolari, refers to the wealth of cultural and spiritual differences among the peoples of the world and the need for each nation to learn from the rest, with which it forms 'God's People'. An extract from John Paul II's encyclical *Redemptoris Missio* calls for a revival in every country of 'the

---

7. A comparison of the pilgrimage booklets distributed to the young people by the various organizing groups and the way each booklet presents the history of Europe would make it possible to present a comprehensive cartogram of the ideological trends (and conflicts) found within French Catholicism. The most significant divergence definitely lies in the way the *Shoah* is (or is not) presented in the various booklets.

missionary epic of the early Church'.

The third and last section is composed of prayers and songs. Interestingly, this part of the booklet contains traditional Catholic prayers which young people can no longer be presumed to know and which were rarely recited in youth movements in the post-conciliar period (Acts of Faith, Charity, Contrition etc., Litanies of the Sacred Heart, the Angelus and so on). It also contains the ordinary of the mass in Latin and a number of songs to the Virgin. The whole deserves a close analysis, but the point needing to be made here is that is expresses a strong desire for (re-)Catholicisation.

Admittedly, the Emmanuel example is not necessarily the best for discovering the character of French involvement in the pilgrimage. However, the triple aim of cultural-religious instruction, accelerated catechesis and Catholic reaffirmation is present in different forms – generally more discreet – in most of the groups and movements present in the organisation of the pilgrimage. This method of instruction in the Catholic identity, carefully prepared in advance by meetings and get-togethers, was powerfully reinforced on the day by the presence among the busloads of pilgrims of large numbers of seminarists, priests and even bishops.

Young People's Interpretations

Faced with this systematic undertaking to reconstruct Catholic memory, it is of course very interesting to examine what the young people themselves have to say about their experience. I limit myself to a few major trends abstracted from the interviews and questionnaire responses in the form of typical expressions which constantly recur – with variants – in the young pilgrims' accounts of their pilgrimage.

The first thing they mention, as the essential benefit obtained from having taken part in the pilgrimage, is the fact of having shared in an extraordinary group experience with other young people: 'It was extraordinary to meet up with so many young people.' This experience of chance meetings, exchanges, shared physical activities and so on transformed an aggregate of atomised individuals into a first person plural with a capacity for collective self-expression – music and song comprising the main vector for this. As an experience of communication within a single age group, it enabled the participants to experience the reality of a common 'youth culture'.

The experience was particularly powerful because it brought together young people from different countries. The 'discovery of new countries' mentioned by most of the respondents is always accompanied by comments about the absence of barriers and frontiers between the pilgrims and the young people living in those countries: 'We discovered that nothing separates us.' 'The main thing was the atmosphere among us, the unity.' 'The people who housed us were wonderful – we felt we all belonged to the same family.'[8] Interestingly, the inherently utopian dream of combining the wealth and diversity of the past to create the Europe of the future is less attractive to young people than the plan to abolish the past by building a 'new world' based on common values of tolerance, mutual respect, hospitality, shared resources, and so on. It is not difficult to see that the meaning given to the 'ethical community' which young people dream of forming – and which they consider they prophesied on their pilgrimage – is deeply rooted in the Christian ethic in which these young Catholics were socialised at an early age.[9] However, the respondents themselves practically never refer to the need for a 're-Christianisation' of Europe as a prerequisite for the social affirmation of their values. The real-world implementation of the Christian dimension immanent in those values seems utterly to absorb their vision of the 'missionary responsibility' which the Pope's invitation was intended to impress on them.

Asked what the gathering meant to them in terms of religious experience, the young people massively stress the personal spiritual progress favoured by the very form of the pilgrimage: 'It gave me a chance to see where I stood.' 'It gave me time to think about my faith.' 'You're on the move all the time, at times you've had your fill, you can't see the point of it all – it's just the same as the search for understanding.' 'It enabled me to make progress in my life of prayer.' This 'personal progress' theme is somewhat accompanied by more critical references to the 'rigidity' of the programme of group prayer meetings and services, or slightly cutting remarks about the excessive directivity of the leadership: 'too

---

8. Which family? The European family? More likely the 'youth' family, it being the privilege of youth culture to erase the divisions stemming from history.

9. The total absence of reference to the political aspects of the formation of such a community is also revealing in this respect.

interfering.' 'They were afraid of silence.' Among the aspects of the pilgrimage which are explicitly censured, the 'lack of freedom' (meaning both 'lack of free time' and 'lack of personal autonomy') is a clear winner. Nonetheless, the presence of the priests was welcomed, that of the bishops in particular: 'we had very explanatory sermons, they were very interesting.' However, 'that wasn't the main thing.' What is massively regarded as 'the main thing' is 'personal testimony' (including that of the priests and bishops). 'the real benefit was the way we exchanged our experiences.' 'When we started telling each other about our personal experiences, something really happened in the group, and we felt the Holy Spirit was amongst us.' The instruction sessions,[10] the scripture readings, the prayer meetings and even the celebrations were ranked as 'high points' of the pilgrimage insofar as they made room for mutual testimony. Similarly, the encounter with the 'major sites' of central Europe is ranked as a 'spiritual enrichment' insofar as it also allowed the pilgrims to meet 'witnesses' with personal experience described as 'strong', 'authentic' or even 'heroic' – the meetings with priests and lay believers who had been sent to prison under the communist regime are often mentioned in the pilgrims' comments.[11]

Compared with the extremely dense and highly emotionalised group experience which was operative throughout the pilgrimage, how did the young people situate the meeting with the Pope? The outstanding feature in both the questionnaire responses and the interviews is the relatively short amount of space given by the respondents to their references to the ceremonies in Czestochowa. The very poor physical conditions encountered – there was considerable overcrowding., and many young people were unable to gain admittance to the gathering – were probably partly responsible for this. The French organisers' wish to avoid any

---

10. Asked about the usefulness of the pilgrimage booklet which they had been given, the young people travelling with a diocesan group said in the first instance that it had been useful for 'the songs and the guitar chords'. The second most frequent response was that it had been useful for personal prayer and 'meditation hints'. Their third most common reference was to its usefulness for taking part in the services.

11. One of the questions on the survey sheet distributed to the young people from this same diocese asked them to list the stopovers which made the deepest impression on them. The responses produced the following rank order: touring Auschwitz, discovering the beauty of Prague, and taking part in ecumenical worship at Taizé.

manifestations of pope-worship may also have played a part in this cool overall attitude – though John Paul II himself is invariably mentioned with warmth and even enthusiasm. Nonetheless, analysis of the responses shows clearly that for the vast majority of the pilgrims the stay in Poland was not the essential aspect of the pilgrimage. To cut a long story short, it would seem that the young people were grateful to the Pope for issuing his invitation, which gave them an opportunity for a group experience which they almost always considered to have been particularly impressive in places other than Czestochowa. For instance, it is interesting that the young people from one diocese, asked what helped to strengthen their feeling of belonging to the Church, mention meeting 'different' Eastern churches on their home ground and their familiar, 'community' relationship with their bishop who travelled in their bus with them. In a very general sense, it appears that direct interpersonal contact and 'local' community encounters were the seedbeds for the decisive identification experiences which the young pilgrims mention spontaneously.

Conclusion

This account of the way in which the young French pilgrims themselves describe their experience of the pilgrimage remains, unavoidably, far too impressionistic. As it stands, I think it calls for three remarks. Firstly, a discrepancy can be discerned between the political and religious utopia implied in the plan for the 'New Evangelisation of Europe' based on the revisited common history and the young pilgrims' prophecy of a new ethical regime liable to find a place in a European homeland stripped bare of the demons of history. Secondly and equally significant is the discrepancy between the cultural discourse concerning the 'Christian roots of Europe' on which a section of the Catholic institution's strategy for the reconstitution of the Catholic identity is based and the almost wholly emotional involvement characterising the young people's relationship with the 'major sites' of European history and culture.

Finally it is clear that young people give primacy to immediate individual and community experience and the subjective expression of this experience, over and above any form of institutional authority governing the relationship of each believer with the line of believers – even when the young people concerned are those whose degree of socialisation in Catholicism is globally much higher than that of other baptised members of their age group.

This triple discrepancy highlights the heterogeneity existing between 'youth culture', denoted simultaneously by an affirmation of the validity of subjectivity and by the immediacy of experience and self-expression, and the cultural and symbolic universe inhabited by the adults responsible for designing the young people's identity training programmes known as the World Youth Gatherings.

Over and above this conflict of generations and cultures, however, what I believe we can detect, almost clinically, is tension between two ideal-typical models of the formation of religious identity, seen here in the Catholic sphere. On the one hand, we have a politico-utopian project and a cultural mobilisation of memory. On the other, we find an ethical prophecy and an emotional mobilisation of memory. It does not strike me as impossible to suggest that corresponding with these two types of modes of formation of religious identity there may also be distinct modes of religious elaboration of a European identity.

11
War and European Identity
Jon Davies

Events in Eastern Europe have dramatised the distinction between state and society; the society *may* underpin the state or it may be in radical disjunction with it. At times of conflict, states may engage in forms of enmity (war) which may or may not be rooted in social identity – wars may be popular or (to use the old-fashioned term) dynastic. States may indeed at times wage war against their own society.

The patterns of enmity reflected in *inter-state* war seem to be remarkably volatile, with the last war's enemy being this war's ally – see, for example, Japan or Italy in the last two world wars, or Italy even during the actual course of the second war. In April 1992, the defence ministers of NATO and what used to be the Warsaw Pact sat down 'in a spirit of partnership' to discuss, amongst other things, joint military exercises (*The Guardian*, 2 April 1992). Patterns of state enmity can be made and unmade relatively easily.

The boundaries of social identity are, however, nothing like so plastic; and this is particularly so when they are reinforced by war and religion. Wars, particularly when fought with mass involvement and mass death, and particularly when they are symbolised by religion, feed back into the slower immanent social identities of which we are all part, where they become part of *who we are*. In Victory, we are who we are because we are here where our fathers died so that we could be here. In Defeat, we are here where we do not wish to be because our fathers were killed by those who now occupy the lands where we should and will be. This bellicognisant attitude is particularly true of Europeans. Christian Europe became both European and Christian through defensive and aggressive wars against, in particular, barbarians and Islam. Europe became 'the West' by a process of military activity which saw it move from occupation or control of 35% of the world's land area in 1800 to 84% by 1924. In Queen Victoria's reign (1837–1901) not a year passed when, somewhere in the world, there wasn't one of her soldiers fighting for her and her Empire. Much of the history of this century is the history of bitterly contested military withdrawal from these empires. Apart from fighting wars on other people's continents (the 'savage wars of peace') we also fought two world wars on our own continent. The phases of our century are defined by reference to war: pre-war, inter-war, post-war. This is not surprising: there were over ten million battle deaths in World War One, for which over sixty million men were mobilised. The French lost 18.2% of men of military age (ages 15–35), the Germans 15.5% and the British 8.8%. No family in Europe was unaffected by this experience, or by the other wars which killed millions more directly in combat or as civilians caught up in war. World War Two, of course, hugely enhanced the range and style of death during war: European women and children died in gas chambers.

War Memorials

The most common form of public statuary in Europe is the war memorial – commonest in the sense of occurring most frequently as well as in the sense of being the most commonly understood. War memorials are one of the most significant twentieth century innovations – in iconography, in epigraphy, in liturgy and in theology. As common European symbols, they are what Auden called 'Parable art.' Auden distinguished between this form of art and 'propaganda' where propaganda is the use of the power over words to persuade people to a particular course of action, while parable art extends our knowledge of good and evil, not in a didactic way, but as message-bearing, clarifying, instructive, a moral rather than an aesthetic form of symbol, making the need for a response both clearer and more urgent (Auden 1935).

War is about death: and war memorials are death memorials, and in some sense they are simply funeral stones. They are more than that, though, they are lapidary witnesses to the urgent need felt by Europe's living not to let the dead die; they are symbols, that is, of active remembrance, not of dismissive nostalgia: they are reincorporations of the dead into the vital cultures of the living.

War memorials discriminate, they parabilise these, *our,* dead – not those, someone else's dead: and while few war memorials that I have seen actually anathematise the enemy, they clearly honour only their own dead. In that sense, then, war memorials reflect and perhaps perpetuate ancient enmities. In as much as there are 'official' or 'state' war memorials, they may also reflect and perpetuate class or other forms of hegemony and be indeed closer to propaganda than to parable. As a matter of record, though, many of our war memorials were and are clearly a product of local 'grass roots' compassion and action. They are genuinely vernacular parables.

War memorials can therefore be read as intensely parochial 'grass roots' expressions of grief and mourning, with very little in the way of triumphalism over and against or even interest in the outside world: or as minatory enmity-freezing symbols, inviting the enemies of the past to remain the enemies of the present and to become the enemies, and by implication the victims, of the future. War memorials are also, of course, intrinsically male objects: they state the paradigmatic expectations of how men, ideally, should behave, and from this paradigmatic statement are derived all the greater and lesser chivalries of proper male manners and of the nature of men's involvement with women and children.

For the purposes of this chapter, I merely note these particular social and boundary-maintaining functions of war memorials. I will concentrate instead on war memorials as religious symbols, ubiquitous in our common European home, where they can be seen as invoking and invigorating a wider collective Euro-Christian social identity which unfreezes ancient (national) enmity and relocates it at the new boundary of difference and conflict, the West versus the Rest. I must emphasise that while 'Europe' is still in all probability too internally riven and too 'new' to be a political *place*, it is old enough and cogent enough to be a religious *cause*.

The boundary of Europe is to be found not so much in conflicts between competing patriotisms or nationalities or continents but between different virtues or values. This shift is well expressed in the war memorial inscriptions at Heriot's Schools, Edinburgh. There the Great War dead are commemorated with the Horatian *dulce et decorum est pro patria mori*, the Second War with the statement that 'their lives they gave for Freedom, Truth and Right'. The move is from simple patriotism to the claim that the deaths in war were sacrifices ('gave') in the service of a set of universal values – 'universal' that is in that they are exemplified in Euro-Christianity.

War memorials represent the most enduring of all answers to the 'what-to-make-of-war? question. There are three options, much in evidence after the Great War: first, the pacifism (nihilism?) of say, the 'war poets' and books and later films like *All Quiet on the Western Front*; second, the revanchism of German war novels and of some ex-servicemen's organisations; and third, the *dutiful* re-engagement with painful necessity of war memorials and actual behaviour in World War Two – neither jingoistic nor triumphalist, but dedicated to the proposition that the worst values of the west were a burden necessarily worth dying for. Such an attitude to war – neither pacifist nor jingoist – seems to me to make casual enmities (casually shuffled and reshuffled alliances and easily entered wars) a thing of the past, but it can also lead to the rather more deadly conflicts of wars of conviction and belief.

The Spanish Civil War and then World War Two reordered the three different responses to World War One, so that the older values are not so much denied as incorporated into a larger vision. This vision is deeply rooted in Christian imagery and mythology.

Freedom, Truth and Right

When read as religious texts – lapidary texts – war memorials have to be seen as expressing a particularly Christian vision of the heroic epic, an epic which of course long predates Christianity, but which is given a distinctive slant in and through the Passion story of Christ and in the various dramatic and liturgical ways in which this story has been, over many centuries, presented to the people of Europe. Of all the stories 'told' in Europe over the Christian centuries it is this Passion story which reaches deepest into the collective culture of Europe: it determines the extent to which the cultural identity of Europe is amenable to being mobilised for conflict and war.

The central theme of the Passion story is that of voluntary, sacrificial death; and this is the theme most commonly found on war memorials and in the Passion liturgies into whose cadences the war memorial dramas so clearly fit. War memorials in the form of Calvaries are quite common. The war memorial at St Hedda's Church, Egton Bridge, North Yorkshire, has the war memorial as the end of the Stations of the Cross arrayed on the outside wall of the church.

The major themes of the Passion story and of war memorials can be listed as follows:

Of Betrayal;

Of Redemptive Sacrifice;

Of Sacrifice and Redemption rendered effective only by Remembrance;

Of Betrayal by Forgetting;

Of Sacrifice seen not just as Dying, but as Not Killing;

Of the Repetitive nature of the Obligation to Die;

Of the Repetitive nature of the Obligation to Remember;

Of Resurrection/Salvation, via Sacrifice, of and for oneself;

Of Resurrection/Salvation, via Remembrance, of and for others;

Of The Universality of the Redemptive Act:

He/They did that *You* [anyone] might Live.

Of The Rectitude of war fought in this way:

'They saw their duty plain. Their lives they gave for Freedom, Truth and Right.'

Greater love hath no man than this, that he lay down his life for his friends.

The word 'gave' is the most common statement on and of our European war memorials: thus in France a memorial describes *Les Enfants de Château-du-Loir morts pour la France*, and similar statements are to be found on German, Italian and Russian monuments. This lapidary theology is what creates the boundary of Europe – and marks it out from the rest of the world. The old enmities are both remembered and transcended, and the memories transfigured into a common memory of a rather grim and sorrowful sense of burdensome duty: One by One

Death Challenged Them, One by One They Smiled in His Grim Visage and Refused to be Dismayed. (Stonehaven, Aberdeen, Scotland).

The extracts from the Anglican Book of Common Prayer on p.145, set side by side with quotations from war memorials, illustrate the cultural transactions between the Passion story and the war memorials. It should be noted that the responses to the priest's hortatory prayer were often spoken by men who were 'about to go over the top', that is to genuinely offer 'themselves' as sacrifice. A 'left to right' reading will identify the common themes, for example the idea that it is by remembrance that 'faith is kept with those who gave their lives as sacrifice', or that life eternal and/or resurrection awaits both those who made such a sacrifice and those who engage in proper acts of remembrance, of which the most salvific is following the example of the sacrificer.

The central British monument to the Great War is of course the Cenotaph – literally the Empty Tomb. While such a symbol pre-dates Christianity, it is clearly very much part of the Passion story – a tomb vacated by a young celibate male, who suffered and died for us all, and whose resurrection, in remembrance, transcends the bodily maiming which was so integral a part of his Passion:

> He was wounded for our transgression, he was bruised for our iniquities: the chastisement of our peace was upon him; and with his stripes we are healed (Isaiah, 53,5).

Just War

The strength of the Passion story is underwritten by, and itself underwrites, the Christian doctrine of the Just War.

Our war monuments are the war memorials of the Just War – not necessarily the war that was actually fought[1] but the wars that have to be fought – if the Sacrifice was not to have been in vain. The Gulf War, 1991–2, Europe's first

---

1. This, given generals and politicians and easy-living and ungrateful civilians, may well have been unworthy of the Dead.

The Priest:
...didst give thine only son
Jesus Christ to suffer death
upon the Cross for our redemption...
who made there (by his one oblation
of himself once offered)
a full perfect and sufficient sacrifice,
oblation and satisfaction for the sins
of the whole world...and did institute
and in his holy gospel command us to
continue, a perpetual memory of that
his precious death, unto his coming
again.
This is my body which is given for
you... This is my blood which is shed
for you.. do this.. in remembrance of
me take this in remembrance that
Christ died for thee..

The People.
We thy humble servants...
offer and present unto thee O Lord,
ourselves, our souls and bodies, to be
a reasonable, holy and lively sacrifice
unto thee..although we be unworthy
through our manifold sins, to offer
thee any sacrifice, yet we beseech thee
to accept this our bounden duty and
service.

The Priest
The Body of our Lord Jesus Christ
which was given for thee preserve thy
body and soul unto everlasting life.
Take Eat this is remembrance that
Christ died for thee

And feed on him in thy heart with
thanksgiving

They died that we might live
(Kilmartin, Argyllshire)
Through the grave and gate of death
we pass to our joyful resurrection.
(Sandridge)
Be thou faithful unto death and I will
give you a crown of life.
(Great Milton, Oxfordshire)

This Calvary was erected by their
Friends. (Kensington)

They gave we have
When you go home tell them of us and
say; for their tomorrow we gave our
today
Greater Love hath no man than this
that he lay down his life for his
friends

These gave their lives that you who
live may reap a richer harvest ere you
fall asleep

They shall not grow old as we that
are left grow old. At the going down
of the sun and in the morning we shall
remember them

In loving memory and sure hope of
life eternal the king of the world shall
raise us up who have died for his laws
unto everlasting life.

Les enfants de Château-du-Loir morts
pour la France.

collective war[2] moved from oil-enmity to Just War precisely by appealing to the Christian roots of Europe and Euro-Christian views of war, as articulated on our war memorials and in the Passion Story of which they are part. Europe may have within it a variety of non-Christian religions: but they are not part of our common European home – our Heimat: that is Christian, not Muslim. Much more problematically it is not Jewish either, but that must remain the subject of more extended treatment elsewhere.

The Just War doctrine derives from a concern of Catholic theologians to cope with the regrettable tendency of Euro-Christian dynasties and proto-states to go to war with each other: it was a doctrine elaborated to facilitate, albeit control, war – not to make it impossible. It now becomes most easily transposed onto those political entities beyond the moral boundaries of the Christian west. The Gulf War was supported by 80% of the British, 70% of the Americans and, as it progressed, by a majority of Germans: and by the Russian government, if not the Russian people, whose views we did not know. Just War doctrine, and the witness of war memorials, both of which, for example, emphasise the propriety of combatant (selected) death *only*, were reflected in the emphasis placed on 'smart' weapons, which met both that criterion (combatant or selected death only) and the doctrine of proportionality – i.e. of military restraint and the use of appropriate means. Smart weapons have the additional theological advantage that the high level of control that they vest in the highest public authority and the relative distance they put between the attacker and recipient increases 'manageability' of the conflict and minimises the danger of face to face 'berserk' behaviour between combatants. The huge expense of smart weapons means that they will be deployed mainly by states, and all other less smart (ie. less discriminating) weapons can therefore be branded as 'terrorist' weapons. Smart weapons are smart theology.[3]

The pulling down of the Berlin Wall ended an eighty year long war in Europe. There has been no serious suggestion of taking advantage of the military weakness of Eastern Europe by attacking it, partly because to do so would run counter to

---

2. 'Rommel, Montgomery, Schwartzkopf – the military pedigree is unmistakeable' (*The Daily Mail*, March 1 1991).

3. They are also mostly ideology – most of the ordnance used in the Gulf war was not smart.

our view of what war is about, and partly because the people of Eastern Europe are part of Christian Europe – no matter how many ecclesiastical differences there may be within the Heimat: 12,000 peace-keeping soldiers were sent to former Yugoslavia. Enmities will generally flow outwards[4] in a series of punitive expeditions directed by a culture which sees the alien and hostile Other beginning where the war-memory of Europe ends: and this boundary, historically, geographically and symbolically, is to be found where our war memorials mark it – with our dead.

Value systems and cultural identities are not as plastic as enmities; but if as and when cultural identities and enmities become associated or synonymous, then there is the clear problem that the next century's wars of 'the West' are likely to be very serious things indeed. Oddly, it may well become the task of the structures of enmity – states, separately or in unison – to put the brake on the bellicose systems of social identity of the West.

---

4. And so half a million soldiers were sent to Arabia.

12

Christianity and the Green Option in the New Europe

Michael Watson

The central question in this chapter is where Christianity stands in relation to politics in the new Europe that has been emerging in the past decade. I am approaching this essentially at the level of political philosophy and political culture, and the tendencies therein, rather than political institutions and processes as these are operating. I am also concerned with Europe-wide developments, though perhaps what I have to say has more bearing at this point in time on the Western half of the continent.

David Edwards (1990) suggests that Europe's most important question today is what the basis will be for its main value system. He puts forward four principal contenders: Christianity, scepticism, Communism and consumerism (as a version of capitalism). He rules out Islam 'as being "foreign" in a profound sense'. Whether or not this view is true, it is necessary to ask what the public and therefore political face of Christianity's claim could take, not in a party political sense so much as in relation to the basic values and beliefs of a major worldview or political paradigm which would significantly shape the nature of the new Europe's politics (and through that, of course, its broader societal character, including its economics).

Mainstream Christian commitment would appear to remain wedded to the defence of liberal democracy, pluralism and the market economy as they currently operate (including the social and welfare 'supplementation' of market economics inherent in liberal democracy). If Christianity continues to be concerned with no more than that, then its likely contribution will be left to Christian Democracy. This would be reinforced by the fact that, as David Edwards has said, 'Most electorates and most politicians in the [European] Community have rejected any idea that there ought to be a profound ideological chasm or class war between "Christian" Democracy and "Social" Democracy' (1990:ch4). The central issue for Christianity and politics would then continue to be the degree to which the 'consumerist version of capitalism' was modified (balanced) by the 'social dimension'.

I accept that a Christian Democratic option *of that sort* is a possible (and may be the most likely) orientation for Christianity's key contribution, ideologically, to European political development. However, another possibility has recently appeared, particularly in the context of the new Europe. It relates to two main developments of the past few years: one, the significant reinforcement of integration in the European Community, starting with the Single Market programme and continuing with the Single European Act and the Maastricht Treaty on European Union; the other, the end of the Cold War, the tearing down of the Iron Curtain, and the collapse of communism in Central and Eastern Europe. But beyond these, in themselves historic key events, there are other perhaps not altogether unrelated but certainly less perceptible developments (less perceptible, at least, in terms of media coverage).

These developments may be summed up in terms of the emergence of a 'New Politics', which is itself associated with such phenomena as post-modernism, post-materialism and transnationalism. Some of the elements in these phenomena may be contradictory to some degree, yet it is appropriate to talk of a 'New Politics' possessing an essential coherence, at any rate in political culture terms. It is as yet rather more a West than East European reality, although an important aspect of it is its post-Marxist character; indeed, in a wider sense, the New Politics does accord with the new Europe as a post-socialist Europe (in the sense of socialism as statist collectivism). However, in the New Politics the downfall of Marxism as the dominant alternative worldview to liberal capitalism cannot be attributed simply to the collapse of communist regimes in Eastern Europe and the Soviet Union. It began altogether earlier in Western Europe, and notably in France, with an ideological critique *from the Left*. Indeed, thinkers like Emmanuel Mounier, Camus and especially Simone Weil had pointed the way from the mid-1930s; but the momentum really gathered pace after 1968 (symbolised by the renunciation of Garaudy, the PCFs 'in-house' intellectual) and issued most significantly in post-modernism in the 1980s.[1]

Post-modernism is a multi-faceted concept, applied in and to many diverse spheres of human life and activity. Its ambiguity reflects the ambiguity and ambivalence inherent in contemporary life. Important for politics is that it does, however, reflect a decisive breakdown of belief in the Enlightenment project or historical assumption of universal Progress based on Reason and in the modern Promethean myth of humanity's mastery of its destiny and capacity for resolution of all its problems. No overarching, universalist claims for a 'best way' can be rationally grounded or justified. As Aronowitz (1988) has put it: 'Most postmodernist discourse is directed toward the deconstruction of the myths of modernism' and leads to 'the renunciation of foundational thought, of rules governing art, and of the ideological "master discourses" (of) liberalism and Marxism.' For Ross, 'Western Enlightenment philosophy... creates a world of universals in order to imagine itself as universal for the rest of the world' (1988:xii) whether in the form of liberal or Marxist humanism or the social democratic variant. The reality is that such 'imagining' was dependent for its plausibility largely on European, then Soviet and American imperial ascendancy, two of which have now disappeared and the third is withering rather fast. The post-Cold War world is polycentric, with diverse political cultures increasingly asserting their particular presence not to say transnational force (in which religion can be a major element – Islam evidently, but also some brands of Christianity e.g. evangelicalism, and Japan's 'Confucian social order' – Gilpin 1987).

However, it may be asked, have we not got the globalisation of capitalism and the world-wide penetration of the market economy? This is true, although some feel there is a tendency towards mercantilism on the part of the major trading

---

1. The term was apparently coined by J F Lyotard (1979).

blocks which may well intensify, thereby obstructing if not reversing the development of global free trade; the major trading powers also seem to be seeking to identify the major corporations with themselves, so slowing and diluting the development of truly multi-national or global corporations. In any case, there is no necessary contradiction, certainly in the sense of a dynamic antithesis, between globalisation and polycentrism in the post-modern conception of contemporary history. Even if capitalism is triumphing world-wide, simply as an economic system, it is not seen as completely determining the political culture or system, the character of a society or the culture of a region. If you like, post-modernist capitalism has a degree of electicism in these respects.

Post-modernism is, indeed, saying that a truly global culture is not to be expected. Capitalism as such cannot create a civilisation or culture in the full sense, but only a dynamic production and consumption process involving a relatively superficial, shifting pattern of tastes and wants. Each political and social space, at least of a certain 'weight', can still assert its own cultural identity – Europe not least. However, is not this sort of analysis accommodating capitalism too much to the post-modernist perspective? Capitalism remains closely associated, not least in its globalisation, with central elements of the modernist 'canon' and helps keep them strongly alive. These elements are rationalisation – which is based heavily on a technical, instrumental conception of rationality – bureaucratisation and technocratic management, deracination (the breakdown of community) and secularisation. Such processes have not, of course, spared politics, far from it, and have had significant consequences for it, such as most obviously centralisation, managerialism and the policy-making emphasis on 'technics' (problem-solving techniques and the technological fix, including the 'selling' of the message or answer). There is also, and most fundamentally, the over-riding commitment to economic growth, which really determines all the ends or 'programmes' that are promoted and largely reduces politics to questions of technical means (especially economic management) and technological development. Politics and ethics are sundered – and religion driven to the margins of public life, at most an irritant, otherwise irrelevant.

The fixation on economic growth has, as Berger (1976) has pointed out, a powerful mythic aspect: it promises a world of freedom and happiness based on abundance. However, the sacrifices required by the processes of modernisation that its pursuit engenders – whether via market capitalism or state socialism – are considerable (summed up by Berger as coming either under a 'calculus of pain' or a 'calculus of meaning'). As a consequence, the mystique progressively loses its capacity to *command* collective and individual allegiances to the disciplines inherent in the modernisation process. A central tenet of modernism, the verification of claims (largely used to some effect against religion), ironically turns on its progenitor: the claims of modernisation can be subject only too well to an empirical balance-sheet and with increasingly informed publics (due to modern education and the media) this becomes the rule rather than the exception in practice. Promises of worldly fulfilment are brought down to earth. Scepticism leaves nothing untouched, not even its greatest creation, techno-scientific achievement. Where comparison can readily operate, the unravelling effect can be that much stronger, as Eastern Europe has shown: communism was not only failing to approach its particular social aims, but in particular, it was proving inferior to its capitalist rival as a mode of economic expansion.

Within the West, capitalism as it (inevitably?) operates, in modernist mode, is not inherently secure either from the ravages of the balance-sheet of scepticism. It has long been recognised that it is not in the business of supplying a moral order. More controversial has been the view that it eroded the moral order or set up a conflict between its modernisation norms, including in the political system, and the values of liberal culture. But in respect of its 'advanced' stage, such interpretations were to be powerfully pushed home in the 1970s by leading writers such as Hirsch (1977), Berger (1976) and in particular Bell (1976). The development of liberal values is not unrelated to the advance of capitalist modernisation, notably in the promotion of individualistic consumerism for marketing purposes. Indeed, Sam Brittan (1973) made the case for capitalism in that it contributed to greater permissiveness as far as the individual was concerned (for Bell, for 'permissiveness' read 'antinomianism'). What the other writers saw, however, was that these tendencies were producing a culture and society out of joint with the requirements of modernisation and in particular economic management (corporate or governmental), as well as subject to an increasing degree of disorder. In such a situation there are likely to be demands for 'remoralisation' (Davies 1987) or enhanced policing.

What the analyses of Bell, Hirsch and others point to is that the economic coherence of the market does not guarantee the cohesion of market society. While Hirsch laments the 'depleting moral legacy', and asks that policy should encourage people to behave 'as if' they were Christians (it is not clear quite how), Bell looks to a full and proper restoration of religion's place – which is to say not in a purely privatised form. For where a view of religion as a private matter is strongest, in the Anglo-Saxon world, it is *there* that is found the greatest disjunction between the social and moral orders on the one hand and the economic order, on the other, as well as the substantial and growing disarray of each (Gilpin 1987 has noted that Japan's economic strength is closely allied to its 'Confucian social order'). These accounts are important in charting the way for the emergence of post-modernism. Latterly, indeed, Bell has been given credit for having 'largely anticipated... many of the leading issues (concerning) modernism, post-modernism, the post-industrial society and the rise of narcissistic consumerism' (Turner 1989:199).

Post-modernism, then, does not appear as a wholesale replacement of modernism but as a demultiplication of it, and the impulse of capitalism's globalisation helps develop this. This fissuring of the modernist monolith particularly brings into question what progress consists of – hence such recent titles as 'Rethinking Progress' (Alexander and Sztompka 1990). That post-modernism continues, however, to articulate modernist themes alongside new or rediscovered non- or anti-modernist ones is shown by one writer's characterisation of a major facet of it as being 'a maximum of mobility and a minimum of history' (Gibbins 1989:xvii). In fact, the only 'mobility' that may be truly post-modern is the ability to think beyond Enlightenment political ideologies and the modernist paradigm itself – and some at least of that involves a recovery of a historical sense. The crucial point, though, is that the weakening of the modernisation project's dominance, as its consistency declines, is linked to the emergence of new political and social forces as well as to the opening up of cultural and ideological 'space' – including the opportunity for the relegitimation of religious language in a public way, given that it speaks to a distinct realm of meaning and values.

Ideologically and politically, the linchpin of the modern undertaking has been national-statism (of a liberal sort) on the European model. Gellner identified its key modernisation contribution in the furthering of what he very aptly called 'social entropy', namely the dissolving of particularistic group identities (notably ethnic and religious) into a larger, culturally homogeneous and secular society. This rationalising action was called forth 'by the objective, inescapable imperative of industrial development' (Gellner 1983). 'Entropy-resistance', while acknowledged, was seen as essentially rearguard if not altogether reactionary. Today, only a decade on, this analysis does not stand up too well empirically or normatively, in the light of post-modernist developments. The nation-state has been under increasingly heavy centrifugal pressures, from above and from below, in the last few years, with its sovereignty much in question. What this reflects above all is the growth of transnational forces and organisations. Some of these are moving the locus of decision-making above the level of the nation-state (transnational corporations and the EC most obviously), some striving – and succeeding to some extent – in pulling it down to a lower level (minority nationalism and regionalism), and some pressing for a movement in both directions (environmentalism and the Green movement). Christianity should be, in many respects, more at home in this situation in Europe, especially if it gives a central role to the ecumenical movement and engages seriously with the major concerns over-shadowing our future, to do essentially with humanity's relations with nature and its place in the cosmos (evidently, of paramount theological significance).

Post-modern development not only presents a greater opportunity for religion to reclaim its role, as the dominance of the modernist framework declines, but also provides substantive orientations in political and social culture which are more convergent with Christian beliefs than the secular ideologies with origins in the Enlightenment. These orientations are to be found in the New Politics, which are closely associated with the New Social Movements, of which the Green movement can increasingly and justifiably claim to be the most encompassing (relating significantly to development and peace issues, minority rights and feminism, besides its basic environmental/ecological concern). The New Politics derive from the development of social and political divisions and re-alignments which cut across the old allegiances. An important shift of attitude and opinion of this sort is that identified by Inglehart from a series of studies in Western countries (notably in the EC) over the past two decades. The new cluster of attitudes is called by him 'post-materialism' and involves a shift of emphasis in people's priorities away from questions of physical or material security, as conventionally defined, to those of the 'quality of life', above all to do with the wider environment (natural, social and cultural). Inglehart writes: 'Less than a generation ago, a materialist consensus reigned... both Marxists and capitalists agreed that economic growth was a good thing.... Today [its] value has been called into question ...' (1989:251).

Post-materialism, Inglehart shows, is related to high levels of affluence and education. Post-materialists are a minority in the EC, but a growing one; on the other hand, materialists are also today a minority, as 'roughly half' of the population do not fall clearly into one category or the other. Between 1970 and 1987 there was 'a substantial increase in the relative proportion of post-materialists' (Inglehart 1989:253). Such people are widening their horizons beyond immediate material self-interest and showing a concern for something beyond the gratification provided by consumer goods. Most, it is true, have not associated this with regular church membership, indeed taking their distance from what is regarded as traditional religion. Most of the church is identified with the 'old' system. The question then arises whether the church's fate, at least since the early middle ages, must always be associated, for the greater part, with the 'old order'; thereby leaving sections of it, at some point, running to catch up with new developments and, to do so, being pushed into reinterpreting their beliefs accordingly (this, surely, has been the relationship with liberalism and socialism – essentially secular ideologies – in the second half of the nineteenth century and the first two-thirds of this century). Such re-interpretation may be valid, but it has by no means always started from a basis in biblical theology and doctrine.

What I believe is special about post-modernist development is that it provides Christianity, if it so wishes, with an opportunity for significant re-entry into the public sphere and consciousness on its own terms. This opportunity is signalled particularly in the phenomenon of post-materialism and in the more specific form of the Green movement. Post-materialism is viewed by Inglehart as an important element in the evolution of post-modernist culture; it may be viewed, indeed, as *the* political element, raising 'new issues and a new axis of conflict' (Ingelhart

1989:251) – one which, as he and others have shown, is gradually replacing the old axis of industrial society (that between Left and Right as defined essentially in late nineteenth or early twentieth century terms). A major question in this situation concerns the adaptability of party systems, but the response of organised Christianity is also likely to be of considerable significance. This is so because, while still part of post-modernist 'deconstruction', post-materialism itself points to a *reconstruction* of the basic value paradigm, largely replacing the dominant modern one. Such reconstruction should be, in principle, more congenial to Christianity than a permanent post-modernist state of fragmentation and rampant relativism.[2] Indeed, it should be positively welcomed when Christian building blocks of beliefs and values can make a basic, and quite probably indispensable, contribution to the whole undertaking.

In the construction and articulation of the new paradigm, the Green movement clearly holds a central place. Much thinking and theorising has already been done by its proponents and considerable progress achieved in advancing policy ideas and influencing the policy agenda. A key unifying concept that has emerged is that of sustainable development, or the sustainable society, to replace the economic growth model as the lodestar of human behaviour and yardstick of policy. However, underpinning this philosophically is a reappraisal of humanity's relations with nature and a critique of anthropocentrism. Both of these undertakings can be amply grounded in the Bible and in the past decade or so the churches and theologians have been doing this. The original catalyst, it seems, was an article by Lynn White, Jnr., on 'The Historical Roots of the Ecologic Crisis', which pointed the finger at the Judaeo-Christian tradition as the source of the problem, in particular through the influence of the Genesis 'story' on man's separation from and dominance over nature, and in promoting his place at the centre of the natural order. There is little doubt that such attitudes, with their associated *hubris*, characterised the development of Western science, technology and economics from the sixteenth century on and were enshrined in Enlightenment philosophy and ideologies. White's interpretation of Christianity's role in this has

---

2. It is these which Bell's cultural contradictions of capitalism, Gellner's social entropy and Hirsch's depletion of the moral capital, clearly breed.

subsequently been brought into question. But, what is more important, there has been a very largely convergent response, from Catholics, Orthodox and Protestants, that Christianity's true meaning in these matters is almost the reverse of that attributed to it by some.[3] That meaning is today summed up in the phrase 'the integrity of creation', which speaks of humanity's responsibility and caring role (stewardship) towards the rest of nature, of a much humbler view of itself as a species in the created order, of its status as trustee and not possessor of the earth, and not least of the wholeness, interdependence (under God) and ultimate glory of the created order. An anthropocentrism does remain, but it is a much qualified and constrained one.

This appears to be a theological recovery of the creation theme alongside that of human redemption which has tended to predominate in much of Western Christianity, perhaps especially since the Reformation. Moreover, each theme is regarded as integral to the other (not one *or* the other) and inter-related, so that in the case of redemption this is for the whole of creation, and Christ has a cosmic dimension. In these writings the role of the Holy Spirit is re-emphasised in sustaining life. The practical commitment to a new, ecologically sustainable world order emerges directly from these 'theoretical' considerations. The crucial need for *metanoia* (total conversion) in our Western way of life is thus rooted in the fundamental, central themes of the Christian faith.

However, the convergence does not come solely from the religious side. On the whole, environmentalism emphasises the importance of the religious dimension, or spirituality, in dealing with the ecological crisis. In his major historical study of the *Roots of Modern Environmentalism*, Pepper sees the Great Chain of Being cosmology of medieval Christendom as substantially in tune with contemporary ecological thought (not least, 'Both animate and inanimate natures were included

---

3. Major contributions have come from the World Council of Churches JPIC programme (since mid-1980s), from Roman Catholicism world-wide (e.g. S McDonagh) and the Holy See, from the Conference of European Churches 1982 Bucharest Consultation on 'The Groaning of Creation', from the Assisi inter-faith gathering in 1986, from the Church of England (2 reports, 1975 and 1986), from the Church of Scotland's 'While the Earth Endures' 1987 report, from the European Ecumenical Assembly in Basel 1989, from the Church in Wales' 'Faith in the Environment' conference report 1990, and from the Ecumenical Consultation organised by the Swiss Churches, 1991.

in the organic conception of the Chain'). He notes that, 'The Soul is the immanent force linking the parts of the whole, and the world is in a way a *single life* stretched out to an immense span and consisting of *linked parts*' (italics in original). He believes that nineteenth century romantics (perhaps some biologists) 'carried forward into twentieth century ecocentrism some of the concepts inherent in the Chain of Being cosmology' (Pepper 1984). In probably the most definitive survey to date of Green political thought, Dobson too brings out the significant spiritual component in it, with reference in particular to such leading figures as Porritt and Winner, Capra and Spretnak, Bahro and Schumacher (Dobson 1990). As early as page 18 he states: 'The Green programme can hardly be understood without reference to the spiritual dimension...' and he notes 'the spiritual asceticism that is so much a part of political ecology.' He quotes Porritt on a key Green political tenet: 'reverence for one's own life, the life of others and the Earth itself'. In Bahro he feels that, 'the missionary sense is never very far away', specifically in Bahro's conviction that 'We need a new Benedictine order'.[4] However, Dobson concludes that there is 'a gulf between spirituality and politics in the... Green movement' and that 'spirituality ought to come to meet the politics'.[5]

Amongst Green ideologists there can, indeed, be awareness of Christianity's significance, though also some hesitation towards it, as it tends to be associated with the 'old' order. Arne Naess, the 'father' of deep ecology, feels that the stewardship approach (to the man-nature relationship) 'moderated, and more closely associated with Christian humility... may contribute to a strengthening of awareness of ecological responsibility. *The religious background for such an awareness is an irreplaceable plus*' (Naess 1989; italics in original). Daly, the 'father' of steady-state economics, in his latest, most wide-ranging work (with Cobb) *For the Common Good*, concludes with a chapter on 'The Religious Vision'. This specifically discusses the Christian and ecological groundings of what it calls the biospheric vision, and emphasises the strengths of theocentrism

---

4. Dubos also plumps for the Benedictine model, though amongst Christians, e.g. Lynn White, there has been support for the Franciscan way.

5. It is noticeable he does not consider the possible role of Christianity in this respect.

in 'under-girding' that vision. Spretnak, in a piece on the 'Spiritual Dimension of Green Politics' (Spretna and Capra 1985), believes they 'should resonate with people who are members of churches, synagogues, temples, etc.' She is 'interested in "spirituality at the (local) level" and in cutting across dividing lines in our pluralistic culture.' Greens undoubtedly have some difficulty in making sense of some inter-denominational (let alone inter-faith) religious divisions that obstruct a convergent, constructive response to the assault on nature. Some Christians for their part have worries about Green connections with the New Age movement. These are probably exaggerated: according to Spretnak, 'in rejecting humanism, Green politics separates itself from much of (that) movement.' In any case, dialogue – ecumenical, inter-faith and amongst 'post-moderns' – would seem to be the moral imperative where humanity and nature (creation) are concerned. Since the Assisi gathering and declarations of leaders of the major world religions in 1986, the World Wide Fund for Nature has been helping to promote this through its 'religion and conservation network'.

Christianity's strengths in responding positively to the current time of crisis and *kairos* are, of course, its still strong roots in European society and in particular its transnational reach. After three or more centuries of a Western monologue, the onus on the West is to conduct a dialogue with the developing world in which it listens first. Christianity is able to show a lead to Europe on this, linking questions of environment and development from its own experience in a way that they need urgently to be linked, and in this joining with the post-materialist forces in Europe. Christianity, too, is surely called to join in the development of an alternative paradigm and society reaching beyond the current post-modern 'moment'. This will involve bringing Creation 'back in' to a central place in our consciousness, not just in terms of respect and care but equally in those of awe and reverence. The latter is, I believe *at the heart* of the recovery of the sacred in Western society which post-modernity heralds. Greens regularly call for such a restoration. Is 'official' Christianity in Europe to miss *this* call of 'groaning creation' (including humanity) – and again leave the response essentially to others?

13
Final Reflections
James A Beckford

I shall orient this concluding chapter towards questions about the meaning of terms such as 'Europe' and 'European' partly because they are far from precise and partly because the reasons for this lack of precision give us clues to the possible future of religion in Europe. Even the spatial extension of the continent is unclear to the North, East and South. Yet, this is rarely a problem for most purposes. Similarly, the political and cultural identities of Europe are, to say the least, indistinct. Yet, this is hardly an obstacle to making claims in everyday conversation about distinctively European practices or institutions. In fact, we can usually tolerate a wide margin of ambiguity and imprecision about things European.

Is this true, however, for *religion* in Europe? This is a more difficult case. The reasons for this difficulty bear on the possible futures for European religion and are therefore worth exploring at some length. My general argument is going to be that there are good reasons for being cautious about phrases such as 'European religion' or 'religion in Europe' but that an examination of the problems associated with these phrases can help to raise useful questions about the future of religion. This is not to argue against the usefulness of categorising things as 'European': it is merely to reinforce Grace Davie's point that Europe is complex and to draw attention to the wide variety of not-always-mutually-compatible assumptions that are made when Europe serves as the framework of any sociological analysis. Indeed, the preceding chapters are excellent evidence for the importance of a focus on the European dimension or background of religion and religious change. But it is nevertheless helpful to expose the diversity of assumptions that their authors have made about the terms 'Europe' and 'European' in their interpretations of religion in the 'common European home'. For the sake of convenience, I shall group my arguments under the headings of history and geography, while recognising, of course, that in practice these two dimensions of social life are strongly intertwined.

History

One possible reason for choosing European religion as a specific topic for analysis is that Europe is considered the site of the historical origins of religious developments which have subsequently been influential in other parts of the world. It is common for North Americans in particular to think of Europe as 'the Old World' and as the progenitor of their main religious institutions. And this is true in some respects. But, in other respects it conceals some important considerations and it distorts the historical record. First, this equation of 'European' with 'original' glosses over the fact that Judaism and Christianity were not European in their origins. Second, it de-emphasises the pre-Christian religions of European tribes and the non-Christian cults of Greek and Roman antiquity. In other words, European religion is much more diverse than is implied by the association with the Old World, Judaism and Christianity. Third, there is a tendency to allow the term 'European religion' to conceal (or to diminish the significance of) the fact that the non-European world has exercised a powerful influence over the development of religions in Europe.

Does it matter that 'European religion' is a less-than-fully-precise, shorthand label for phenomena which did not actually originate in Europe, which are not representative of the full spectrum of the religions that have developed on European soil, and which have been shaped in part by forces from outside Europe? For most purposes, it does not matter at all. But it becomes an important matter when considering the *future* of religion in Europe. Why?

If the tribal origins of Judaism and the close association that developed in Late Antiquity between Christianity and tribal chiefdoms are recalled, the persisting imbrication of religion, ethnicity and early modern nationalism in many parts of Europe should not be too surprising. It may be convenient or comforting to believe that 'old' tribal and ethnic boundaries or enmities have no place in the late twentieth century, but Judaism and Christianity took root in many places in Europe via the medium of just such social forms. The association between them is not therefore accidental or incidental. It was eventually eclipsed in most of Western Europe by power structures based on social class, social status and the nation-state. But in other places, religious identity has remained inseparable from quasi-tribal and ethnic groupings which may still reassert themselves or may be imposed by enemies if other power structures are weakened, as in the collapse of Soviet hegemony in Central and Eastern Europe. For example, the Catholic heritage of Lithuania and the Ukraine was the primary vehicle for the nationalist sentiment which fuelled the movement against Soviet communism in the 1980s. Similarly, the internecine struggle between rival nationalisms in Armenia and Georgia follow religious lines of division in part. By contrast, Estonia's Lutheran heritage has not served as the symbolic or material basis for anti-Soviet resistance (Johnston 1993). In other words, it is helpful to look back at the history of the social forms which have 'carried' Christianity and Judaism if we are to grasp clues about their future.

David Martin's claim that religion played an 'eminent role' in the overthrow of communist regimes in Central and Eastern Europe after 1989 is fully justified. But religion is *also* associated with deep-seated enmity and communal violence in many places, notably in the former Yugoslavia, parts of the CIS, Ireland and wherever anti-semitism and hostility to Muslims occur. It is therefore naïve to think of these disorders as exceptions to the European rule simply because they cannot nowadays be attributed to the old battles between the Catholic and Protestant churches. The fact is that tribal and ethnic divisions were integral to the initial growth of Judaism and formative of the development of Christianity in Europe. If socio-economic or political conditions permit, these divisions can either re-emerge or be re-invented, as in contemporary Armenia and Georgia.

Moreover, the future of religion in Europe may be bound up with traditions which are not simply rediscovered: they can be reappropriated by means of thoroughly modern ideas such as subjectivity or personal identity (Hervieu-Léger, 1993). There is a possibility, then, that religion will serve as either a catalyst or a carrier of ethnic divisions expressed in modern ideological idioms. An early test of this possibility will occur in Russia, according to Petya Nitzova, and in some other countries where young people are beginning to learn for the first time about Orthodox Christianity. Will they simply reproduce the religion of their grandparents? This is less likely than the possibility that they will selectively meld elements of Orthodox spirituality with elements of the kind of privatised, transcendent humanism (Lambert 1986) which spread with market-led industrialisation and urbanisation in Western Europe.

The possibility of a closer articulation between religion and ethnic divisions in the future of Europe, East and West, will become stronger if the popularity of single-issue politics and new social movements continues to increase. The mobilisation of concerns about, for example, peace, racism, human rights, regional sovereignty, and ecology outside the frameworks of political parties and parliamentary politics has been gaining momentum for more than two decades. At the same time, the major Christian churches and Jewish organisations have been meeting more and more challenges to their formerly privileged position to speak authoritatively on religio-moral issues. As a result, new social movements and campaigning groups of all kinds have begun to draw independently on religious symbolism and values to support their cases without necessarily operating through the channels of religious organisations (Beckford 1989). The very structure of the European Community's bureaucracy and the relative weakness of the European Parliament make it correspondingly easier for single-issue campaigns, lobbies, interest groups and movements to influence policy and resource allocation. In this way, minority cultures and regions, with or without aspirations to ethnic distinctiveness, have paradoxically benefited from the growing centralisation of the European Community's functions and institutions. At the same time, the resurgence of nationalist sentiments in formerly communist countries is evidence of a deep-seated ethnic divisiveness which had been temporarily held in check by pseudo-modern totalitarian regimes. The opportunity to participate in European and global markets has reinvigorated particularism and, as in the case of

Lithuanian and Slovakian nationalism, drawn heavily on a Catholic heritage. These trends do not suggest that closer political relations between European states will be reflected in pan-European religious imagery. Fragmentation on the religious level seems more likely to parallel political and economic integration, as Richard Roberts implies.

It is not therefore surprising that Jean-Paul Willaime regards the organised Protestant voice in European politics as weak. The very willingness of many Protestant churches to work cooperatively with political parties and campaigns in the past may ironically have hastened the transfer of religio-moral legitimacy to parties, trade unions and social movements which no longer need or seek the churches' blessing. The formal differentiation between religious and political institutions is sharper in areas of Protestant influence, but my point is that the symbols and values of Reformed Christianity remain 'available' to campaigners. Michael Watson's chapter, for example, traces the increasingly tangled web of affinities and connections between Christianity and ecological movements. The future of religions in Europe is likely to depend in part on the uses to which their reservoirs of meanings and motivations are applied in political and social movements independently of the formal religious organisations.

It seems unlikely, however, that, with the possible exception of Islamic political parties, Europe of the future will have any powerful political parties with a religious base. The force of Christian Democracy is already in decline in Western Europe, although the afterglow of 'diffused' Catholicism may continue to shape Italian politics, for example, for a long time (Cipriani, 1989). Even in countries like Spain and Poland where the Roman Catholic Church was patently active in bringing about a transition to democratic government, relations between churches and government are unlikely to remain cordial for very long (Giner 1992). Patrick Michel's view is that Poland's new-found democratic pluralism will probably have a more corrosive effect on Catholicism than did many decades of communism. This is particularly likely to happen if officials of the church fail to realise that their role is now to withdraw from direct involvement in politics.

> When Polish country pastors (and the occasional bishop) instruct their congregants in precisely which political party to support in free elections, the Church is not only making itself look foolish: it is jeopardising its

capacity to play its most important political role in consolidating Polish democracy, which is precisely a *pre*-political role. (Weigel 1992:198)

Indeed, an interesting test of the Catholic Church's commitment to pluralistic democracy is already taking place in countries where it now faces competition from new religious movements for the first time. There have been signs of religious intolerance and repressiveness in Hungary and Poland since 1989. It also remains to be seen for how long there will be popular support for Christian Democracy in Slovakia and Hungary once the Church's history of opposition to communism begins to fade from memory.

Geography

Just as the history of so-called European religion can be a useful guide to the future if sufficient attention is given to tribal and ethnic underpinnings, so the continent's apparently taken-for-granted geographical integrity also provides some clues to future developments. But the meaning of these clues requires careful interpretation. Admittedly, there is widespread agreement that the outer limits of Europe are the Arctic, the Mediterranean and the Urals, leaving aside such marginal cases as Greenland or Malta. My argument is more basic. It is that the geographical origins of things European are not necessarily the most straightforward guide to their future. In other words, many religious phenomena which originated within the geographical boundaries of Europe have subsequently been shaped by so many influences from outside the continent that their future depends at least as much on non-European considerations as on European ones.

Take the case of Roman Catholicism. This church is in many respects a quintessentially European institution in its origins and historical development. Yet, some of the trends which currently seem likely to characterise Catholicism's foreseeable future stem from other parts of the world as well as from Europe. The influence of Africa, Latin America, the USA and Asia is plain to see in post-Vatican II developments in ecclesiology, economic ethics, the status of the laity, and forms of worship. Indeed, the case could be made that, although the centre of Roman Catholicism's power remains in Rome and that this is most unlikely to change under Pope John Paul II, the church's centre of gravity is already shifting to North America and the Third World. Indeed, the circulation of 'surplus' European priests through Latin America and the USA is generating strong pressure for ideological and organisational changes for which there is relatively little call in Europe. There may come a point at which it will mean little to describe the Roman Catholic Church as European.

It would be more difficult to sustain the same argument with respect to the main Protestant churches of Western Europe, although there is no doubt that pressures for change in the Church of England derive at least as much from the worldwide Anglican communion as they do from the UK. Similarly, the experiences of communities of Methodists, Baptists, Presbyterians, Congregationalists and the smaller British denominations outside Europe have been particularly influential in inspiring and shaping ecumenical initiatives. One of the reasons why British Protestant churches have been relatively slow to become active in European circles is that they have been oriented more towards other regions of the world than towards Europe. The World Council of Churches has therefore been a more important forum than any European grouping, at least for the relatively liberal-minded among the UK's Protestant denominations.

The case for being cautious about the importance of a narrowly European focus on the future is reinforced by consideration of the evangelical and fundamentalist movements, churches and campaigns which have already had a major impact in Central and Eastern Europe since 1989. The impetus for the high-profile and well-resourced campaigns to recruit conservative evangelicals all over Europe comes mainly from the USA, Latin America and East Asia. Of course, European churches are cooperating with these campaigns, but most of the drive to evangelise the countries of the former Soviet sphere of influence has non-European roots. By comparison, the competing and halting efforts of Western European Protestant federations to influence Central and Eastern Europe are relatively ineffectual for the reasons stated by Jean-Paul Willaime. It is conceivable, therefore, that large numbers of people in the 'new Europe' could be converted to forms of Protestantism which bear relatively few European characteristics. American evangelists who harness the technology of satellite broadcasting and video production are most likely to succeed in their aims of 're-converting' Europe.

This possibility raises a more general question about Europe's religious creativity in the future. The continent has given birth to some of the world's most influential religions and religious organisations, but will it be more of a *receiver* than a donor in the future? The most influential sectarian movements in European Christianity have come from the USA since the mid-nineteenth century (Jehovah's Witnesses, Christian Science, Mormonism and Seventh-day Adventism); the roots of Pentecostalism also lie in the USA; and the charismatic renewal which affected even Roman Catholicism can be traced back to American origins. The picture for Judaism is not quite so clear, but the various movements to strengthen Orthodoxy which have been effective in recent decades have undoubtedly benefited from American and Israeli support. This may be partly why Régine Azria queries whether postwar European Jews constitute a self-conscious and homogeneous entity, except by reference to *Shoah*. Moreover, very few of the new religious movements which began to attract a following in the 1960s were European inventions. In short, much of the present-day religious vitality in Europe is a selective response to non-European stimuli. The future of religion will therefore reflect this apparent imbalance in the geographical sources of innovation. On the other hand, Danièle Hervieu-Léger's analysis of recent Catholic campaigns to 're-evangelise' Europe rightly emphasises the possibility that young people may be capable of adapting their religious heritage in a creative fashion which could cut across national and ethnic divisions.

We are left with the paradox that, whereas levels of religious practice and the extent of religion's significance for public life are declining in most of Western Europe and Scandinavia, the continent's boundaries are becoming more sharply defined in religious terms. Europe is perceived to end at the point where Islam begins, despite the fact of Turkey's constitutionally secular status. The demise of Soviet-inspired hostility to organised religion has only served to accentuate the uniqueness of Islam's role as Europe's boundary. This is not, of course, a new situation, but the salience of the geographical boundary (or, better, frontier) with Islam is heightened by the growing importance of Muslim minorities *inside* a number of Western European countries. The collapse of Yugoslavian federalism into religiously identified nationalisms which pit Muslims, Catholics and Serbian Orthodox Christians against each other has also sharpened popular images of Islam as 'the other'. The long-running tensions between Turkey and Armenia,

Greece and Turkey, as well as between Christians and Muslims in Albania and Bulgaria, are warning signs that the struggle for political power in these regions continues to follow religious fault lines. The outcomes will also help to shape the future of religions in other parts of Europe where the dress codes of Muslim schoolchildren or the status of Muslim women in their own households are framed as questions of pluralism or toleration: not life-and-death communal conflicts.

In sum, the future of religions in Europe is predictable partly in the light of what is known about the tribal and ethnic forms in which Christianity and Judaism were originally established and partly in the light of evidence about the influences emanating from outside the continent's geographical boundaries. History and geography provide the best guidance, although in both dimensions there is a need to be cautious about the reasons for taking Europe uncritically as the frame of analysis for religion.

Bibliography

Abbott, N. 1985, *Aisha, The Beloved of Muhammed*, Al Saqi Books, London

Abd Al Ati, H. 1977, *The Family Structure of Islam*, American Trust Publications

Abrams, M., Gerard, G. and Timms, N. (eds) 1985, *Values and Social Change in Britain*, London: Macmillan

Acta Apostolicae Sedis, 1931, Vol. 23

Adonis, A. and Tyrie, A. 1990, *Subsidiarity: an history and policy*, London: Institute of Economics Affairs

Aganbegyan, A. 1988, *The Challenge: the economics of Perestroika*, London: Hutchinson

Al-Ghazaly, M. (n. d.), *Kay Naf'ham Al-Islam, Dar'al-Kitab Al-Hadith*, cited by Al-Mana 1981

Al-Mana, A. 1981, 'Economic Development and its Impact on the Status of Women in Saudi Arabia', Ph.D. Thesis, University of Colorado

Alexander, J. C. and Sztompka (eds) 1990, *Rethinking Progress*, London

Andrews, A. Y. 1990, 'Women's Rights in Islam', unpublished paper given to the Islamic Society, School of Oriental and African Studies, London

Appignanesi, L. and Maitland, S. 1989, *The Rushdie File*, London: Fourth Estate

Aretin, K. O. von, 1970, *The Papacy and the Modern World*, London: Weidenfeld and Nicholson

Arnold, J. R. 1992, 'Eine Konsultation in Basel: Erwiderung auf zwei Vortrage', *Oekumenische Rundschau*, 41 (1): 76ff.

Aronowitz, S. 1988, 'Post-modernism and Politics', in A. Ross (ed) 1988

Ash, T. G. 1989, *The Uses of Adversity*, Cambridge: Granta Books

Ash, T. G. 1990, *We The People: the Revolution of 89*, Cambridge: Granta Books

Ashford, S. and Timms, N. 1993, *What Europe Thinks: a values handbook*, Aldershot: Dartmouth

Auden, W.H. 1935, 'Psychology and Art Today', in S. Hynes 1976, *The Auden Generation*, London: The Bodley Head

Beckford, J. 1989, *Religion in Advanced Industrial Society*, London: Unwin Hyman

Bell, D. 1976, *The Cultural Contradictions of Capitalism*, London: Heinemann

Belloc, H. 1962, *Europe and the Faith*, London: Burns and Oates

Berger, P.L. 1976, *Pyramids of Sacrifice*, London: Faber and Faber

Birge, J. G. 1937, *The Bektashi Order of Dervishes*, Hartford, Conn.

Blanquart, P. 1987, 'Le pape en voyage: la géopolitique de Jean-Paul II', in P. Ladrière and R. Luneau (eds), *Le retour des certitudes*, Paris: Centurion

Brenner, B. 1990, 'Dienende oder dominierende Kirche?' *Le Messager Evangélique*, 43, 28 October

Brierley, P. 1991, *Christian England*, London: Marc Europe

Brierley, P. 1991, *UK Christian handbook 1992/93*, London: Marc Europe

Brittan, S. 1973, *Capitalism and the Permissive Society*, London

Bruce, S. 1986, *God Save Ulster!: the religion and politics of Paisleyism*, Oxford: Clarendon

Camps, M. 1965, *Britain and the European Community 1955–1963*, London: Oxford University

Castles, S., Booth, H. and Wallace, T. 1984, *Here For Good: Europe's new ethnic minorities*, London: Pluto

Castoriadis, C. 1975, *L'institution imaginaire de la Société*, Paris: Seuil

Cecchini, P. *et al.* 1988, *The European Challenge: the benefits of a single market*, Aldershot: Wildwood House

Cipriani, R. 1989, '"Diffused religion" and new values in Italy', pp. 24-48 in J. Beckford & T. Luckmann (eds) *The Changing Face of Religion*, London: Sage

Clarke, P. 1988, 'Islam in Contemporary Europe', in S. Sutherland *et al.* (eds) *The World's Religions*, London: Routledge

Coulson, N. and Hinchcliffe, D. 1978, 'Women and Law Reform in Contemporary Islam', in Beck & Keddie (eds), *Women in the Muslim World*, Cambridge: Harvard University

Dahrendorf, R. 1990, *Reflections on the Revolution in Europe*, London: Chatto and Windus

Daly, H. and Cobb Jr., J. B. 1990, *For The Common Good*, London

Daniel, N. 1960, *Islam and the West: the making of an image*, Edinburgh

Daniel, N. 1975, *The Arabs and Medieval Europe*, London: Longman

Daniel, O. 1990, 'The Historical Role of the Muslim Community in Albania', *Central Asian Review*, 9 (3)

Davie, G. 1990, 'Believing without Belonging: Is this the future of religion in Britain?', *Social Compass*, 37: 455–69

Davies, S. 1987, 'The Remoralisation of Society', in M. Loney (ed), *The State of the Market*, London

Dawisha, K. 1988, *Eastern Europe, Gorbachev and Reform*, Cambridge: Cambridge University

Dawson, C. 1932, *The Making of Europe: an introduction to the history of European unity*, London: Sheed and Ward

Dawson, C. 1948, *Religion and Culture*, The Gifford Lectures, London: Sheed and Ward

Dawson, C. 1952, *Understanding Europe*, London: Sheed and Ward

De Sousa Santos, B. 1989, *The Post-modern Transition: law and politics*, Coïmbra: Centro de Estudos

Djait, H. 1985, *Europe and Islam*, translated by Peter Heinegg, Los Angeles and London: University of California

Dobbelaere, K. 1985, 'Wordt het pausbezoek meer dan een groot volksfeest?', *Dietsche Warande en Belfort*: 428–434

Dobson, A. 1990, *Green Political Thought*, London

Dray, S. W. 1980, *Perspectives on History*, London: Routledge and Kegan Paul

Dubied, P-L. 1990, 'A propos du contenu de la (ré)évangélisation de l'Europe', in Faculté Universitaire de Théologie Protestante de Bruxelles, *Protestantisme et construction européenne*, Actes du Colloque des Facultés de théologie protestante des pays latins d'Europe, Brussels: Ad Veritatem

Edwards, J. 1988, *The Jews in Christian Europe*, London: Routledge

Edwards, D. L. 1990, *Christians in a New Europe*, Manchester

EECCS 1991, *Maastricht et l'aprés-Maastricht*, Brussels

European Community 1973, 'The European Identity', *Bulletin of the European Communities*, 12: 118–22

Fadhl-Allah, Marim Nor Al-Deen. 1977, *Al-Marah fe Dhelal Al-Islaan*, Beirut: Daral-Zahra

Featherstone, M. (ed) 1990, *Global Culture: nationalism, globalization and the world system*, Binghampton NY: State University of New York

Fédération des Eglises Protestantes de Suisse 1990, *Europe, Europe occidentale, Suisse. Réflexions Protestantes*, Berne-Lausanne: Institut d'Ethique sociale de la Fédération des Eglises Protestantes de Suisse

Fédération Protestante de France 1991, *Pour quel monde? Eléments d'information*, Paris-Strasbourg: Les Bergers et les Mages-Editions Oberlin

Fukuyama, F. 1991, *The End of History and the Last Man*, London: Hamish Hamilton

Galland, O. 1991, *Sociologie de la jeunesse*, Paris: Armand Colin

Gellner, E. 1983, *Nations and Nationalism*, London

Gilpin, R. 1987, *The Political Economy of International Relations*, Princeton: Princeton University

George, G. S. 1967, 'Subsidiarity', *New Catholic Encyclopaedia*, 13: 7623

Gibbins, J. R. (ed) 1989, *Contemporary Political Culture*, London

Giner, S. & Saraza, S. 1992, 'Sviluppo politico e Chiesa in Spagna', in Aa.Vv. (Various Authors), *La Religione degli Europi*, Turin: Fondazione Giovanni Agnelli, pp.101–53

Gluck, C. 1985, *Japan's Modern Myths: ideology in the late Meiji period*, Princeton, NJ: Princeton University

Gorbachev, M. 1988, *Perestroika: new thinking for our country and the world*, London: Collins

Habermas, J. 1991, *Citizenship and National Identity*, Brussels

Haddad, R. M. 1986, 'Eastern Orthodoxy and Islam: an historical overview', in N. M. Vaporis (ed), *Orthodox Christians and Muslims*, Brookline, MA: Holy Cross Orthodox Press

Halsey, A. H. 1985, 'On Methods and Morals', in M. Abrams *et al.* (eds)

Hanson, E. O. 1987, *The Catholic Church in World Politics*, Princeton: Princeton University

Harding, S., Phillips, D. with Fogarty, M. 1986, *Contrasting Values in Western*

Europe, London: Macmillan

Hasluck, F. W. 1929, *Christianity and Islam Under the Sultans*, Oxford: Clarendon

Hastings, A. 1986, *A History of English Christianity*, London: Collins

Heino, H. 1991, *Churchgoing and Churchgoers in Finland*, Pieksämäki: Finnish Lutheran Church, B Series, No.69

Herrin, J. 1987, *The Formation of Christendom*, Oxford: Blackwell

Hervieu-Leger, D. 1986, *Vers un nouveau christianisme*, Paris: Cerf

Hervieu-Leger, D. 1993, *La religion pour memoir*, Paris: Cerf

Hobsbawm, E. and Ranger,T. (eds) 1983, *The Invention of Tradition*, Cambridge: Cambridge University

Hubner, K. 1985, *Die Wahrheit des Mythos*, Munich: C. H. Beck

Hughes, H. S. 1952, *Oswald Spengler: a critical estimate*, New York

Inglehart, R. 1989, 'Observations on Cultural Change in Post-Modernism', in J.R. Gibbins (ed)

John Paul II, Pope 1980, 'Cyril and Methodius' and 'Egregiae Virtutis', in *The Pope Teaches*, 4 (1–3), London: Catholic Truth Society

John Paul II, Pope 1985, *Europe and the Faith*, Address to the European Bishops' Conferences, London: Catholic Truth Society

Jenkins, K. and Smart, M. 1990, *An Open House? The European Community: looking to 1992*, London: British Council of Churches/Council of Churches for Britain and Ireland

Johnston, H., 1993, 'Religio-nationalist Subcultures under the Communists: comparisons from the Baltics, Transcaucasia and Ukraine', *Sociology of Religion*, 54 (3): 237-55

Kees, I. 1960, *Die europäische Christenheit in der heutigen säkularisierten Welt*, Nyborg

Kaufmann, F. X. 1988, 'The Principle of Subsidiarity viewed by the Sociology of Organizations', *The Jurist*, 43

Komanchak, J. A. 1988, 'Subsidiarity in the Church: the state of the question', *The Jurist*, 43(6)

Ladrière, P. 1989, 'La vision européene de Jean-Paul II', in R. Luneau and P. Ladrière (eds.)

Lambert, Y. 1986, *Dieu change en Bretagne*, Paris: Cerf

Lane, D. 1990, *Soviet Society Under Perestroika*, London: Unwin Hyman

Lehman, A. G. 1984, *The Euorpoean Heritage: an outline of Western culture*, Oxford: Phaidon

Lerman, A. 1989, *The Jewish Communities of the World*, London: Macmillan

Lerner, G. 1986, *The Creation of Patriarchy*, London: Oxford University

Levy, R. 1957, *The Social Structure of Islam*, London: Cambridge University

Lewis, B. 1976, *Studies in Classical and Ottoman Islam: 7th -16th centuries*, London: Variorum Reprints

Lortz, J. 1959, *Europa und das Christentum*, Wiesbaden
Löwith, K. 1949, *Meaning in History*, London
Luneau, R. and Ladrière, P. (eds) 1989, *Le rêve de Compostelle*, Paris: Le Centurion
Lyotard, J-F. 1979, *The Post-Modern Condition: a report on knowledge*, Manchester: Manchester University
Martin, D. 1978, *A General Theory of Secularization*, Oxford: Blackwell
Mehl, R. 1959, *Das protestantische Europa*, Stuttgart
Mernissi, F. 1975 *Beyond The Veil*, Massachusetts: Schenkman
Michel, P. (ed) 1985, *Religions et Société en France: problemes politiques et sociaux*, La Documentation Française, 518
Michel, P. (ed) 1992, *Les Religions à l'Est*, Paris: Cerf
Michel, P. 1991, *Politics and Religion in Eastern Europe*, Oxford: Polity
Minai, N. 1981, *Women in Islam: tradition and transition in the Middle East*, John Murray Publications
Mughniyyah, A. M. J. 1986 and 1987, 'Marriage According to the Five Schools of Islamic Fiqh', *Al-Tawhid*, 4 (1 & 4) and 5 (1–4)
Mughniyyah, A. M. J. 1988 and 1989, 'Divorce According to the Five Schools of Islamic Fiqh', in *Al-Tawhid*, 6 (1–2)
Müller, H. 1988, 'The Relationship between the Episcopal Conference and the Diocesan Bishop', *The Jurist*, 43: 116–118
Mutahhery, A. M. 1982, *The Rights of Women in Islam*, Tehran: Islamic Seminary
Naess, A. 1989, *Ecology, Community and Lifestyle*, Cambridge
Nell-Breuning, O. V. 1957, 'Solidarität und Subsidiarität im Raume von Sozialpolitik und Sozialreform', *Sozialpolitik und Sozialreform*, Tübingen
Nicholl, W. and Salmon, T. 1990, *Understanding the European Communities*, New York
Nielson, J. 1992, *Muslims in Western Europe*, Edinburgh: Edinburgh University
Nora, P. 1984, *Les Lieux de Mémoire*, Paris: Gallimard
Novak, M. 1989, *Catholic Social Thought and Liberal Institutions*, New York: Transaction Publications
O'Connell, J. 1991, *The Past and Future Making of Europe*, Peace Research Report 26, University of Bradford: Department of Peace Studies
Peet, R. 1991, *Global Capitalism: theories of societal development*, London: Routledge
Pepper, D. 1984, *Roots of Modern Environmentalism*, London
Pfeffer, K-H. 1957, 'Der Protestantismus in Europa: Dokumente', *Zeitschrift für internationale Zusammenarbeit* 13: 171–4, 183–278
Pirenne, H. 1939, *Mohammed and Charlemagne*, New York: W. W. Norton and Co.
Piwowarski, W. 1975, 'Le principe de subsidiarité et l'Eglise', *Collectanea Theologica*

Pochet, Ph. 1991, 'Construction Européenne. Subsidiarité: la bouteille à encre', *Revue Nouvelle*

Rahim, A. 1911, *The Principles of Muhammadan Jurisprudence*, Lahore

Ramet, P. (ed) 1989, *Religion and Nationalism in Soviet and East European Politics*, Durham, NC: Duke University

Reeber, M. (1991) 'A study of Islamic Preaching in France', in *Islam and Christian – Muslim Relations*, 2 (2), Birmingham: Centre for the Study of Islam and Muslim–Christian Relations, Selly Oak, Birmingham

Rendtorff, T. 1977, 'Universalität oder Kontextualität der Theologie: einer "europäische" Stellungnahme', *Zeitschrift für Theologie und Kirche*, 74: 238-54

Rey, J. 1973, 'Die christlichen Kirchen und die europäische Integration', in H. Uhl (ed), *Europa: Herausforderung für die Kirchen*, Frankfurt am Main: Otto Lembeck Verlag, pp.9–19

Robertson, R. 1979, 'The Golbalization Paradigm: thinking globally', *Religion and Social Order*, 1: 207–24

Robinson, F. (1988), *Varieties of South Asian Islam*, Centre for Research in Ethnic Relations, University of Warwick, Research Paper No.8.

Roser, H. 1979, *Protestanten und Europa*, Munich

Ross, A. (ed) 1988, *Universal Abandon*, Minneapolis

Roussel, L. 1989, *La famille incertaine*, Paris: Editions O. Jacob

Runciman, S. 1982, *The Medieval Manichee: a study of the Christian dualist heresy*, Cambridge: Cambridge University

Rushdie, S. 1988, *The Satanic Verses*, London: Penguin Viking

Sahas, D. J. 1971, 'The Seventh Century in Byzantine-Muslim Relations: characteristics and forces', *Islam and Christian–Muslim Relations*, 2 (1)

Sahas, D. J. 1972, *John of Damascus on Islam: the heresy of the Ishmaelites*, Leiden: E. J. Brill

Said, E. 1978/91, *Orientalism: Western conceptions of the Orient*, Harmondsworth: Penguin

Schwartz, J. 1980, *Katholische Kirche und Europa: Dokumente 1945-79*, Munich/Mainz

Séguy, J. 1971, 'Une sociologie des sociétés imaginées: monachisme et utopie', *Annales ESC*, March–April: 328–54

Shaw, A. 1988, *A Pakistani Community in Britain*, Oxford: Blackwell

Sklair, L. 1991, *Sociology of the Global System: social changes in global perspective*, London: Harvester

Southern, R. W. 1962, *Western Views of Islam in the Middle Ages*, Cambridge, MA

Speelman, G. E. 1988 in J. Slomp, G. E. Speelman and De Wit, *Muslims in the Netherlands, Muslims in Europe*, Research paper No.37, Birmingham: Centre for the Study of Islam and Muslim–Christian Relations, Selly Oak Colleges

Spengler, O. 1926, *The Decline of the West: form and actuality*, London: George

Allen and Unwin

Spengler, O. 1932, *Der Mensch und die Technik*, Munich

Spretnak, C. and Capra, F. 1985, *Green Politics: the global promise*, London

Spinka, M. 1933, *A History of Christianity in the Balkans: a study in the spread of Byzantine culture among the Slavs*, Chicago

Stoetzel, J. 1983, *Les valeurs du temps present*, Paris: Presses Universitaires de France

Stowasser, B. F. 1987, 'Religious Ideology, Women and the Family', in B. F. Stowasser (ed), *The Islamic Impulse*, London and Sydney: Croom Helm

Swatos Jr., W. H. (ed) 1989, *Religious Politics in Global and Comparative Perspective*, New York: Greenwood

Thanvi, A. 1990, *Bahishti Zewar*, 7th ed., Delhi: Dini Publications

Thanvi, A. (n.d.), *Imdad al-Fatawa*, vol. 5, India: Deoband

Thils, G. 1986, *En dialogue avec l'Entretien sur la Foi*, Louvain: Ed. Peeters

Timms, N. 1992, *Family and Citizenship: values in contemporary Britain*, Aldershot: Dartmouth

Tohmar, A. H. 1977, *Al-Syeda Isha*, 2nd. ed., Beirut

Troeltsch, E. 1912, *Protestantism and Progress: a historical study of the relation of Protestantism to the modern world*, London: Williams and Norgate

Troeltsch, E. 1922, 'Das Problem einer objektiven Periodisierung', part 3 of 'Über den Aufbau der europäischen Kulturgeschichte', ch. IV of *Historismus und seine Probleme*, Vol.1, Tübingen

Turner, B. S. 1989, 'From Post-Industrial Society to Post-Modern Politics', in J.R. Gibbins (ed)

Walz, H. H. 1955, *Der politische Auftrag des Protestantismus in Europa*, Tübingen

Watt, W. M. 1972, *The Influence of Islam on Medieval Europe*, Edinburgh: Edinburgh University

Watt, W. M. 1991, *Muslim–Christian Encounters: perceptions and misperceptions*, Routledge: London and New York

Weigel, G. 1992, *The Final Revolution*, New York: Oxford University

Willaime, J-P. (ed) 1991, *Strasbourg, Jean-Paul II et l'Europe*, Paris: Cerf

Willaime, J-P. 1990, 'État, Éthique et Religion', *Cahiers Internationaux de Sociologie*, 88

Wilpert, C. 1986, 'Religion and Ethnicity: orientations, perceptions and strategies among Turkish Alavi and Sunni Migrants in Berlin', in T. Gerholm and Y. Lithman (eds), *The New Islamic Presence in Western Europe*, London: Mansell

Worsley, P. 1964, *The Three Worlds: culture and world development*, London: Weidenfeld and Nicholson

Wright, A. D. (ed) 1982, *The Counter-Reformation: Catholic Europe and the non-Christian world*, London: Weidenfeld and Nicholson

Index

Abbott, Nabia 81
abortion 4, 41
abortion in Poland 36–38
Adonis and Tyrie 116
Aisha 81
Albania xi, 9, 13, 16, 44, 48, 168
Andrews, Ahmed vii, xii, 78, 86
Anglicans and Europe 105
anthropocentrism, biblical critique of 156, 157
anti-semitism 18, 60, 68, 69, 72, 74, 162
Aronowitz, S 150
Azeris 11, 12, 14
Azria, Régine vii, xii, 66, 167
Balkans ix, 44, 46–49
Beckford, James vi, vii, xiv, 54, 160, 163
Bektashi doctrine 48
Bell, D. 152, 153, 156
Benedict of Nursia 20, 129
Berger, P. 151–152
Bishops conferences and papal power 117–121
different planes 119–120
Bishops and leaders meeting (Budapest 1992) and the ten theses 100–102
Bogomil heresy 47–48
Bohemia 38
Book of Common Prayer and war xiv, 144–145
Bosnia-Herzegovina 13
Bosnia and the Muslims 49–50
Briand, Aristide 29
Britain
and Europe 28
Brittan, S 152
Bruce, Steve 2, 97
Bulgaria vii, xi, 7, 9–13
Bulgarian Qizilbash 48
Camps, Miriam 28
capitalism, markets
and the moral order 153, 156
Carmel of Auschwitz affair 76
Castoriadis, C. 118, 119
Catholic heritage and nationalism 162
Catholicism 3
and European Commission 104–105
and Slovak nationalism 41

in Hungary 40,41
Catholics
in Britain 62
in Europe 94
in France 62
CCEE (*Conseil des Conférences Episcopales d'Europe*) 98
Cenotaph xiv, 144
Central Conference of the Methodist Church for Central and Southern Europe 100
Central Eastern Europe 34, 41
and democracy 41
religion and politics 34–35
CEPPLE 99–101
Christendom 18–23
Christian Democracy 149, 164, 165
Christian Democrat party
in Hungary 41
Christian Democrats 96
Christianity and Green option 148–159, 164
Christianity and ethnicity 162
Christianity in Europe 3, 159, 162
Christians and Muslims 168
church and state in France 63
church attendance
motives for 5
services content 5
ritual 5–6
Churches
and Christianity 15
and communism 36
and ethical independence 10
and government in Spain, Poland 164–165
and nationalism 10
and religion 9–11,35
Cipriani 164
Communism 3
difficulties in Eastern Europe 35
Concord of Leuenberg (1974) 100
Conference of the Churches of the Rhine Valley 99
Coudenhove-Kalergi, Richard 29
Coulson and Hinchcliffe 80, 81
cuius regio 94
culture 6
Cyril and Methodius 21–22, 129
Czechoslovakia 5,9, 38, 40, 41